They Played with a Quiet Mind

D1225535

THEY PLAYED WITH A QUIET MIND

CHARLES F. KEMP

Including conversations with

Roland Harper

**Senior Golf Professional
Colonial Country Club
Fort Worth, Texas**

CBP Press
St. Louis, Missouri

© Copyright 1991 CBP Press

Library of Congress Cataloging-in-Publication Data

Kemp, Charles F., 1912-
     They played with a quiet mind / Charles F. Kemp.
1. Golf—Psychological aspects.   I. Title
GV979.P75K455   1991   796.352'019   90-19539
ISBN 0-8272-3627-1

Printed in the United States of America

This Scottish seaside wasteland of heather, whinny, grass, and sand is where it all began...this fascinating, infuriating, this annoying, absorbing game of golf.

St. Andrews Home of Golf

TABLE OF CONTENTS

Section II Qualities of Character of Those Who Played with a Quiet Mind

Preface

They Played with a Quiet Mind

It was said of Ralph Waldo Emerson that he had "the serenity of solitude in the midst of a crowd." Emerson lived before John Reid and a few friends played the first round of golf in America on Washington's birthday in 1881, but he had the attitudes that great golfers have possessed when they were playing their best. It is an attitude all good golfers try to attain.

The synonym for serenity is "tranquility." Indeed the great Harry Vardon once said, "In golf you need above all things to be in a tranquil frame of mind."

A professor of English literature once said, "There is no great art without serenity." Golf is an art form. A golfer who plays the game at its best is an artist just as much as a maestro on the concert stage or a painter before the canvas.

Wisdom of the Fairways

Putting is more art than science.

Ben Crenshaw

The late Davis Love II, formerly head instructor for *Golf Digest* Instructional Schools, was speaking to a group at one of the schools about the intangibles of golf. Among other things he said, "You must put the mind at ease so the body can perform."

I have never forgotten that statement. Great golfers have amply demonstrated it. They have called it by different names but it means the same thing. Fuzzy Zoeller calls it "putting the mind at rest." Paul Bertholy, successful teaching pro, says, "Man, a most emotional creature, functions best when the mind is not in turmoil."

Ben Crenshaw calls it having an "uncluttered mind." The year that he won the Masters he said that in any major tournament there are at least ten players who are capable of winning, and the difference between first and tenth is amazingly small. It is not the swings but the attitudes that determine the outcome. As he put it, those who win have an uncluttered mind. As Davis Love II put it, they have learned to put the mind at ease so the body can perform.

Wisdom of the World

Keep the conscious mind quiet.

Ernest Jones
famous teacher of a
generation ago

Sports psychology is relatively new, but this experience is as old as the game itself. We quoted Harry Vardon who said that above all one must have a tranquil frame of mind. It was about the time that Vardon was winning so many tournaments in England that a man by the name of Arnold Haultain wrote a book called *The Mystery of Golf*, in which he said "golf requires...a mind absolutely imperturbed, imperturbable."[1]

The word "imperturbable" describes the play of Joyce Wethered, the first of the women superstars, who won so many tournaments in England. In fact her biographer said she won more by her imperturbability than by her skill with the clubs.

Ms. Wethered was a contemporary of Vardon and was often compared to him both in her swing and in her attitudes.

They both seemed unconcerned about the outcome of a match, their opponent's score, or anything else. Some said it almost bordered on indifference. It doesn't mean they were careless, it doesn't mean they didn't play to win. It meant that they put their minds at ease so their bodies could perform. In other words, they played with a quiet mind.

Tom Watson described his feeling in the 1982 Open, which he won. He said there came a point where he "felt a great inner calm." He said it was one of those rare moments that only come once in a while, but when it comes it is a great feeling.

This is not something that is limited to superstars in major tournaments. According to Amy Alcott, who has done so well on the LPGA tour, amateurs can experience it as well. Speaking directly to average golfers, she said, "When you were playing well you probably weren't trying to impress anyone, you weren't thinking about results, you weren't thinking about much of anything. Your mind," she said, "was quiet."

There is that term again. Even amateurs can attain it. Does this mean amateurs can score as well as Tom Watson or Amy Alcott? Of course not. They have neither the talent nor the experience of these superstars. It does mean that they can acquire those attitudes of mind and spirit that will help them play according to their full potential.

In 1987 Robert Wrenn, not so successful nor so well known as Watson, was struggling a bit. He just hoped to finish in the top 125 and keep his card for another year. He had not cashed a check of more than $4800, had missed eight cuts since the first of the year, but in the Buick Open he shot 26-under and came within one stroke of tying the record for a low tournament held by Ben Hogan and Mike Souchak. He explained it in these words: "That week I just had peace of mind...I went into the week feeling very calm." Could he do this very often? No, but this time he did. He played with a quiet mind and played the best golf of his career.

David Ogrin, in an article in *Golf Digest*, pointed out that golf is more than having a good swing. If that was all there was to it then the good swingers would win all the tournaments. But they don't. The difference is in their ability to control their emotions. It was their attitudes that determined the outcome. As he put it, "Emotionally they chose to be peaceful and trust themselves." The two key words in that sentence are "they chose." It is a matter of choice. "The truly great players," he says, "can choose to be peaceful."[2]

There are many things that can contribute to achieving the ability to play with a quiet mind. The rest of this study is an evaluation of the experiences of great golfers, past and present, and the things they have done that have enabled them to play with a quiet mind.

If you will read through the Table of Contents you will gain an outline of what these things were and are. I have not used the traditional one- or two-word chapter titles. I have used entire sentences that give a fuller picture of the content of the chapter.

I think it would be of interest to provide some background for the pages that follow. There are several features that make this study different from most books in golfing literature.

• Several years ago I became aware that most books on golf instruction said golf was more mental than physical, then proceeded to discuss the grip, stance, and swing and other physical requirements and only gave a few sentences or paragraphs to the mental side of the game.

In an attempt to fill this void, I studied the thoughts and attitudes of great golfers, past and present, and published them in two books, *Smart Golf*[3] and *The World of Golf and the Game of Life*.[4] These two books were somewhat unique in that they combined the historical with the contemporary approach.

Since these publications over ten years ago, I have continued my studies of the thoughts and attitudes of great golfers. I have discovered much more material, plus the fact that the growing specialty of sports psychology has given us many new insights into the mental side of the game.

This is not a rewrite of the former volumes but a new and much broader approach that preserves the historical and contemporary perspective.

• A lifetime of public speaking and personal professional counseling has caused me to select qualities and ideas from some of the world"s greatest thinkers to help the people to whom I have spoken or with whom I have counseled. It occurred to me that much of this general wisdom about life has direct application to golf. Sometimes these references are included in the text; sometimes they are inserted under the heading "Wisdom of the World."

• While the golfing quotes and illustrations come, of necessity, from great and famous golfers, my main purpose is to help the average—even beginning—golfers. In order to meet this need, I consulted Roland Harper, Senior Golf Professional at Colonial Country Club in Fort Worth, Texas— home of the annual Southwestern Bell Colonial Invitational. He is not only an excellent teacher but a wise student of human nature. In his almost forty years as a teaching pro, he has helped thousands of students develop their games. A few years ago, he and I collaborated on a little book, *How to Improve Your Golf Game.*[5] We dealt almost entirely with the physical part of golf. We did it in a conversational format. It had many good reviews, and one of the most frequent comments referred to the conversational style. It occurred to me that it would greatly enrich the historical and contemporary material if I could include a few conversations with Roland as to how the experiences of these great golfers apply to his students.

It is always a puzzle to know how to use the pronouns "he" and "she." Since golfers are both men and women, I wanted to be fair. In the original manuscript I included "he or she" every time it was indicated. My editor felt that this made for awkward reading, which certainly is true. He suggested that we eliminate constant use of "he or she," and on some occasions use the masculine and on some the feminine pronouns. This certainly makes for easier reading. We trust that all readers will realize that when we say "he" we also mean "she," and vice versa.

I would like to express my appreciation to three friends, each of whom made a significant contribution to this project. I am grateful to Roland Harper, my own golf instructor, who has helped me to understand both the physical and the mental aspects of the game. I appreciate his willingness to share in two conversations which are included in the body of the material. His long and successful teaching career adds a note of authority to what I had to say in other chapters.

I am grateful to Hal Sutton, a very successful touring pro who has encouraged my writing over the years and was kind enough to evaluate the whole manuscript in transcript form. I quote from a letter which he wrote after he had read the material. "...during my most recent trip to Japan I read the entire manuscript and must give it rave reviews. It was excellent and I feel the material would be very beneficial to golfers of all categories."

I am grateful to my friend David Polk, the editor of CBP/ Chalice Press, whose careful editing of the material refined it for final publication and who helped design the cover and the format in such an attractive final product.

To these three friends I own a great debt of gratitude for their help and encouragement. They helped me to attain more of a quiet mind as I approached the time for publication.

[1]Arnold Haultain, *The Mystery of Golf*. Applewood Books, 1908, p. 43.
[2]*Golf Digest*, September, 1987, p. 47.
[3]Charles Kemp, *Smart Golf*. Bryant-Smith, Inc., 1974.
[4]Kemp, *The World of Golf and the Game of Life*. CBP Press, 1978.
[5]Charles Kemp and Roland Harper, *How to Improve Your Golf Game*. Chisholm Publishing Co., 1986.

Introduction

en Assumptions About Playing with a Quiet Mind

As the title indicates, this is a study of the mental and emotional side of golf. It is based on ten assumptions.

1. All golfers are looking for that "winning edge," that indefinable something that enables them to attain their full potential.

2. After a golfer has acquired a knowledge of the basic fundamentals and gained a reasonable mastery of the physical or mechanical skills of golf, the winning edge is in the mind and the emotions.

3. The place to study any area of achievement is in the lives and experiences of those who have demonstrated success in their own experience—in this case, in the lives of great golfers past and present.

4. The same principles that apply to tournament champions apply to the weekend golfer—to a lesser degree, to be sure, but the amateur can learn from the professional in the mental game as well as in the physical game. Just as the amateur patterns her swing and her stance after the champi-

ons, so she should pattern her thoughts and attitudes after those who have been highly successful.

5. The most effective attitude for winning golf is what we have chosen to call a "quiet mind." It is a freedom from tension and pressure, a sense of calm and serenity.

6. Playing with a quiet mind will accomplish two things. It will help one score better and enjoy the game more. Both are important. Both are objectives of this study.

7. A study of serenity and peace of mind can be found in many places: in the writings of poets and philosophers, theologians and psychologists, even in the scriptures. Some quotations from such sources are included in the body of the text and often in inserts in boxes.

8. What applies to golf applies to other areas of life as well. To attain a quiet mind off the golf course helps one to apply it on the golf course. To learn the secrets of playing with a quiet mind on the golf course helps to apply it off the golf course.

9. No one ever obtained a quiet mind in a hurry. No one ever experiences it all of the time. Not even the saints were able to do that. It is a rare attitude that comes and goes. To the degree that these great players were able to master it, to that degree they played well.

10. Playing with a quiet mind is a quality that can be attained. It is not something that is limited to the brilliant or to those with great athletic skills. It does require certain conditions. One must follow certain principles, one must have patience and persistence, but it is available to all.

How others have done this is the subject of this study.

Several years ago, Rabbi Joshua Leibman wrote a book entitled *Peace of Mind*. It became an immediate best-seller, probably indicating how many people desire peace of mind. In the opening paragraph he recounted an experience he had as a young man. He decided to draw up a list of what he considered to be the good things of life. He included such items as health, love, beauty, talent, power, riches, and fame.

When his list was complete, he proudly took it to show to an older man who had been his mentor and role model as a youth. He admitted he was trying to impress him with his wisdom and breadth of interests. The older man looked at the list, read it carefully, and said that it was good but that he had forgotten the most important item of all. He said there was one more ingredient without which none of the others had value. A little crestfallen, Liebman asked him what that might be.

The older man took a pencil, crossed out all the good things he had listed, and wrote three words: "peace of mind."[1]

Let's take that illustration and apply it to golf.

There are many ways to improve one's golf game: take lessons, go to a golf school, study instruction books, watch tapes, watch great golfers at tournaments or on TV, but, most of all, practice extensively and intelligently. All of these are good; in fact, some of them are necessary if one really wants to improve. Like the young man's list, they all have much greater value if, with the lessons and the practice, one also learns to play with a "quiet mind."

The phrase, a "quiet mind," occurs frequently in the pages that follow. In fact, it will appear in almost every chapter. If that seems overdone, it is to emphasize that this one theme runs through all of these varied and different discussions.

Some names appear more frequently than others. That is because some golfers have published more than others, some have won more than others, some have been interviewed more than others, and some have spoken more clearly about the intangibles of golf than others. For this reason, such names as Hogan, Nicklaus, and Palmer appear over and over again because they demonstrated these principles. Also, they talked about them and their quotes are applicable to almost every area discussed. I have tried to provide a balance between great golfers of the past and also some present-day golfers who are just now coming into prominence. To understand the experiences of the giants of history, I have scoured the biographies and histories of the game as thoroughly as possible. To keep the information up-to-date, I read all the golf journals, listened to post-tournament interviews, and read golfers' statements in the newspaper after every tournament.

It is my hope that a study of the thoughts and attitudes of great golfers and some of the quotations from other fields will help you, the reader, achieve those attitudes that will help you play better and enjoy it more—because you have learned to play with a quiet mind.

[1]Joshua Liebman, *Peace of Mind*. Simon and Schuster, 1946, pp. 3f.

How Great Players Have Attained A Quiet Mind

Section

With a fine sea view, and a clear course in front of him, the golfer should find no difficulty in dismissing all worries from his mind, and regarding golf, even if it may be indifferent golf, as the true and adequate end of man's existence.

The Honorable J. J. Balfour

1

They Had Quiet Conversations with Themselves

Plato, the ancient Greek philosopher, called thinking an "inner dialogue." Modern psychologists and psychiatrists say that not only do we do this all the time but it has a major impact on how we feel and act. Some call it "self talk." Others call it "inner speech," or even "internal sentences." Whatever they call it, it all means the same. This inner dialogue, this inner speech, not only influences life in general but has a major impact on what happens on the golf course. If a golfer wants to play with a quiet mind, one of the first things he must do is control his internal sentences.

Thoughts always precede feelings, and thoughts consist of words and sentences. If we think inferior thoughts, we will feel inadequate. If we say angry words to ourselves, we will feel hostile. If we say positive things, we will feel confident. Always, thoughts precede feelings. The secret to controlling feelings is to control the thoughts that result in the feelings, and to monitor the words and sentences that express the thoughts so that we will obtain the kinds of feelings we desire.

9

This is what I call the "internal sentence theory" of golf. It is what golfers say to themselves that determines how they feel and how they play. This can be both a negative and a positive influence. In the World Series of Golf at Firestone, back in 1964, Bobby Nichols came to the par-five sixteenth hole. He had a good drive and a good second shot. All he had left was a one hundred-yard approach shot over a pond to the green—not too difficult for a golfer of his level of play. He said to himself, "If I don't hit this shot just right, it could fall into the water"—which is exactly what it did.

Not many who read this will play in the World Series of Golf, but the same principles apply. If a golfer says such things as "I hope I don't get in the sand," or "This isn't fair," or "I hope I don't miss this putt," or any one of a hundred other negative things one could say, then negative results are almost certain to occur.

The encouraging thing is that one can just as well make positive statements. From *Jack Nicklaus' Playing Lessons* comes a quote that clearly illustrates this theory. He describes an experience he had when he was playing in the 1967 U.S. Open at Baltusrol. "I made a dumb bogey on ten and suddenly was full of self doubt, even though I was still leading by three shots. I'd found many times before when fear started to hit me that my best chance of overcoming it lay in facing it squarely and examining it rationally. Often I do that by actually *talking to myself*. Here's what I said inside my head at Baltusrol. 'O.K. what are you frightened about? You've obviously played well or you wouldn't be here. You're still playing well overall. You're always telling yourself you get your biggest kicks out of the challenge of golf. Well go ahead and enjoy yourself. Play each shot one at a time and meet the challenge.' It worked then and it has calmed me down many times since. I believe a similar sort of internal pep talk might also help you."[1]

Johnny Miller, in an interview in *Golf* magazine, was asked how he maintained composure under pressure. He said it all depended on how he *talked to himself*. He could say, "I have to hit this shot, all these cameras are on me, everybody in the country is watching, I've got to hit it." But if that were his approach, he went on to say, then "I've had it. Instead I want to say something like this. 'You can hit that shot but if you don't it's not going to kill you.'"

He also referred to average players and the problem that confronts them when they have a bad lie. "Most people," he said, "look at a bad lie and say, 'I'm so unlucky,' or 'That was a terrible break and it's going to cost me plenty.' Right away they're dead. But if they say 'Man that's an interesting lie, I wonder what I can do from here,' they'd have a chance."[2]

Amy Alcott, who has done so well on the LPGA tour, also says she talks to herself. She was playing in the Tucson Open. Some of the game's best players were in contention—Pat Bradley, Hollis Stacy, Kathy Whitworth, Nancy Lopez. That's enough to make anyone nervous. She started the final day with what appeared to be a very ordinary round. A bogey on the sixth hole set her back. It was then she began to *talk to herself*. "You don't need to be down. You are a good player. Let's go. Get tough. Let us see what happens. You're the best player out here." What happened was that she birdied the next three holes, as well as the twelfth, and went on to win.

Others also testify to the value of talking to themselves. Hale Irwin, three-time winner of the U.S. Open, said in a post-tournament interview, "I always *talk to myself*. It keeps me loose." David Graham, whose dramatic victory in the 1981 U.S. Open was a tribute both to his skill with the clubs and calmness under pressure, said afterwards, "I actually *talk to myself* on the course. If I have a putt to win the U.S. Open, everybody is screaming, the TV cameras are going, and the world is on fire. I have to keep reminding myself to keep doing the things I always do."[3]

Bruce Crampton was playing in a senior tournament at Chester Valley Golf Club in suburban Philadelphia. He found himself in a play-off with Billy Casper. Casper had just missed a winning putt on the eighteenth hole, giving Crampton a second chance. He said the greens were very difficult to read, and he had had problems with them all day. Now he had a three-foot putt to win, which he made. When he was asked if he had any thoughts of missing that putt on the first play-off hole after seeing Casper miss on eighteen, Crampton answered, "No, that's negative thinking. Golf at our level is played unconsciously. I told myself to be brave. I decided where I wanted the ball to go and I went ahead and stroked it." Crampton has a good putting stroke, but what he *said to himself* enabled him to use it effectively.

Dr. David Morley, the psychiatrist who has made an extensive study of golf and golfers, makes a statement that fits right in with the "internal sentence" theory. "We've all seen golfers," he wrote, who get "caught up in this convulsion of frustration. Some of its agony would have been unnecessary, if the golfer had taken charge of his *internal dialogue*. The golfer who talks to himself in the right way operates from the basic premise that, above all else, he is human, which gives him the right to make mistakes. And that's what a golfer really must do—deal with his own humanness." [4]

In summary: Golf is a target game. From the tee the target is the fairway, from the fairway the target is the green, on the green the target is the cup.

> The target is the goal.
> The ball goes to the target.
> The club propels the ball.
> The hands control the club.
> The arms swing the hands.
> The body supports the arms.
> The mind controls the body.
> The thoughts control the mind.

The thoughts consist of words and sentences, sentences that we say to ourselves. That is the internal sentence theory of golf.

The great golfers may not have been very good at making speeches, but they knew how to talk to themselves.

[1]Nicklaus, *Jack Nicklaus' Playing Lessons*. Golf Digest Books, 1981, p. 56.
[2]*Golf*, June, 1982, p. 48.
[3]*Golf Digest*, September, 1981, p. 42.
[4]David Morley, *The Missing Links.* Atheneum, 1976, p. 152.

All italics in the quotations in this chapter are the author's.

2

They Focused Their Minds on
Positive Thoughts

In the early 1950s a Methodist preacher by the name of Norman Vincent Peale published a book entitled *The Power of Positive Thinking*. It immediately became a best-seller and Peale's name became a household word. It is safe to say that no religious book was read by as many golfers as was this book. There were other books that were also very popular. Dr. Maxwell Maltz, a plastic surgeon, wrote a book called *Psycho Cybernetics*, which had much to say about one's self-image. He contended that people are all goal-seeking beings and they tend to become the way they see or think about themselves. This was also read by many golfers.

These are not necessarily new ideas. William James, the pioneer psychologist in America, spoke of a "stream of consciousness" that flows through everyone's mind. All persons have the power to choose that on which they will focus their attention. An old Yoga philosophy said, "You are what you think." Many such quotations could be added. What they all agree on is that the power of thoughts is one of the most significant facts about any person. When the thoughts are positive they produce one result. When they are negative they produce another. This is such an accepted fact in psychological circles that it needs no further proof or evidence.

As stated above, golfers have given attention to such messages, none any more so than Gary Player. When Johnny Miller was speaking to the golf team at his alma mater, BYU, he used Player as the best example he could think of as a positive thinker. He said Player might have an 82 (a bad round for him) but he would find something positive about it.

Player admits that he is an eternal optimist. He has read and re-read Peale's book on positive thinking. He says when he gets up in the morning he has a choice. He can think positively or negatively. He chooses to think positively.

Davis Love II said to a group of us at one of the *Golf Digest* schools that, when he and Player were both on the tour, Player gave him a tip that increased his earnings by a thousand dollars a week. The tip was: "Never leave the scene of a shot without a positive idea." If it has been a good shot the thoughts are naturally positive. That's good, and he can go to the next shot with confidence. If it has not been a good shot, he stays and takes practice swings until they feel good before he goes on to another shot. If you will watch him on TV as he plays in senior tournaments, you will note that he still does so.

It is no wonder that when Player came to write his own book he called it *Positive Golf*. His formula can be summarized under three headings. First, you have to want to win. Second, you have to believe you can win. And third, you have to think only positive thoughts.[1]

Arnold Palmer is another disciple of the positive thinking doctrine. When he was the dominant player on the tour, his attitude was reflected in his statement, "I never saw a hole I couldn't birdie." His positive approach influenced the attitude of others. One of his contemporaries said, "We used to try to par every hole. When Arnie came on tour we had to try to birdie every hole."

Before the term "the power of positive thinking" became so popular, good golfers were doing it. When Walter Hagen arrived at a tournament, he would take his stance on the first tee, wink at the gallery, and say, "I wonder who will come in second this time." There wasn't a doubt in his mind he could win—and usually he did. They say he was never short on putts because he was sure he could make them, but if he missed one he was sure he could make it coming back.

When good golfers deviated from these positive attitudes they did not play as well. Billy Casper had a great career during the late 60s and early 70s. He won the Open twice, the Masters once, plus a lot of other tournaments. In 1972 he had what was a bad year for him. He said it was not faulty technique—the swing was the same—but he slipped in his ability to concentrate positively. As he put it in an interview, "On a drive I would not positively select a target area. On an approach shot I would not positively decide which club I needed. On an approach putt I would not positively decide the amount of break or the speed of the green. The result too often was an indecisive stroke and a double bogey."

I was once counseling with a college golfer. His coach said he wasn't living up to his potential. I asked him where he was losing strokes. He said "short putts." I asked, "What do you think of when you're over a four-foot putt?" He said, "I think of how embarrassed I would be if I missed." It is reminiscent of Ben Hogan's statement, "I don't mind missing a shot but I don't like to miss it before I hit it."

There are innumerable other examples that could be cited that testify to the all-importance of a positive attitude. Good golfers are aware of this so much that it sometimes borders on superstition. Chi Chi Rodriguez, for example, won't mark his ball with a coin with the tail side up—that is negative thinking. All good players and all good instructors agree: "If you don't think you can make a shot, you probably won't." If you do, you have a much greater chance of accomplishing it. The attitude is reflected in the swing.

Wisdom of the World

The golfer must always find good things to say to himself on the golf course. The flow of positive thinking must never cease. [2]

David Morley,
psychiatrist

If there is one thing that can be learned by studying the experiences of those who have excelled, it is that a positive mental attitude is necessary to play one's best golf. It also is a primary factor in learning to play with a quiet mind. Developing positive attitudes is not as easy as it sounds. The players mentioned above practiced developing a positive attitude as much as they practiced their swing until they could depend on both their attitudes and their swings. A repeating swing and a positive mental attitude: This is the combination for winning golf and playing with a quiet mind.

[1]Gary Player, *Positive Golf*. McGraw Hill, 1967, p. 17.
[2]David Morley, *The Missing Links*. Atheneum, 1976, p. 150.

3

They Were Relaxed in Both Body and Mind

Dr. Edmund Jacobsen of the University of Chicago made some interesting studies of relaxation. He took people into his laboratory and trained them to relax by progressively relaxing each muscle group in the body. As they learned to relax the muscles of the arms, the legs, the trunk, the entire body, they found that they were reducing, even eliminating, some physical symptoms and were also reducing anxiety. In his book, *You Must Relax*, he said, "It is physically impossible to be nervous in any part of your body if in that part you are completely relaxed."[1] Counselors and psychotherapists have been doing this for years. There is a psychological axiom: "You can't be tense and relaxed at the same time."

Relaxation reduces fatigue, renews energy, reduces anxiety, increases physical performance—all the things that are necessary for a good golf swing.

Dr. Richard C. Proctor, of the department of psychiatry at the Bowman Gray School of Medicine, wrote an article in the *1974 PGA Book of Golf*. He contrasted the mental attitudes necessary for sports such as football, basketball, or boxing with golf. He referred to a term frequently heard in all sports: "being psyched up." Being psyched up, he said, is fine for football players, boxers, or track stars. That is especially true in football where a player wants to overpower the opponent. In golf, however, he points out, it is completely different. In fact, it is just the reverse. In golf, he says, "You've got to be relaxed, in complete control of yourself and your emotions. You can't be psyched up and relaxed at the same time, and in golf it's the one with the relaxed swing who is going to have success."[2]

Fuzzy Zoeller, one of the few pros who really seems to enjoy the game, expressed the same idea. But instead of comparing golf to football, he contrasted the golfer with the weight lifter. When he was interviewed after his surprise win in the Masters the first time he played in it, he said, "It's hard to play golf like a weight lifter. He has to get all tightened up to shine. You can't do that in golf. Your whole being has to be relaxed if you are to play this game well."

Tom Nieport and Don Sauers conducted a survey of several leading professionals as to what they felt were the most significant mental factors in golf. Their findings indicate that the pros they interviewed felt that the ability to relax is one of the most important factors of all. The reason was that they felt the ability to relax is so closely related to confidence. In fact, they felt that the two were almost synonymous. They help each other. The player who is confident finds it easier to relax. The player who is relaxed can be more confident.[3]

Arnold Palmer says basically the same thing. In all of his writing he says much about concentration, but he sees a close relationship between concentration and relaxation. In his words, good golf consists of a combination of "intense concentration and total relaxation."[4]

This is an emphasis that the sports psychologists make all the time. Bob Rotella, the dean of sports psychologists, advocates that a person spend some time every day doing relaxation exercises such as Jacobsen trained his patients to do. (Jacobsen went through a rather elaborate program of relaxing the muscle groups one at a time, which is effective but very time consuming.

More recently, psychologists have found they can greatly streamline this by simply having clients or a patient relax one muscle group after another until the whole body is relaxed.) When a person has learned to relax at home she can take this attitude to the golf course.

Those who are skilled at such a procedure can relax on command when they feel themselves tensing up.

Others use other methods. Byron Nelson, Bob Toski, and Jim Flick, in their instruction books, advocate deep breathing as a way to relax. Whenever a golfer feels tense, they advise taking a few deep breaths before continuing. David Graham and Bruce Devlin, two Australians who have won big in America, say this is especially effective in putting. Bruce Devlin, speaking of putting, says it doesn't make much difference what grip or stance is used, so long as the body is relaxed. When the body is tense, it reduces touch. When the body is relaxed, it increases the touch one has with the putter.[5]

There are still other methods. Lee Trevino would banter with the crowd. Bobby Jones would try to lengthen and slow down the backswing. Julius Boros would slow down the pace. Jack Nicklaus and Johnny Miller would remind themselves that it is only a game. Nelson also suggested that a golfer who feels rushed and tense should slow down the feet. Whatever method one uses, relaxation is always beneficial.

Gary Player summarized it when he said that to play competitive golf, one must be relaxed in mind and body. The two support each other. A relaxed mind produces a relaxed body, a relaxed body produces a relaxed mind. Both are essential, whether it is tournament golf or a relaxed weekend foursome. When one is relaxed in both mind and body, then she, or he, can play with a quiet mind.

Professional golf is a pressure-packed game, played before large crowds, even national TV audiences, for huge sums of money. It is a game of intense competition where one pushed shot or a missed putt can cost thousands of dollars, maybe even a tournament. Furthermore, this is not only for a sixty-minute time period as in some games but goes on day after day, week after week, which can take both a physical and emotional toll.

In her thorough study on the *Psychology of Sport*, Dorcas Susan Butt writes, "Stress is the psychological villain of the sports world. It can take away the joy of sport and leave sad and defeated athletes of all ages."[6]

Those who would maintain a quiet mind not only need to relax on the golf course but at times they need to relax off the course as well. For average golfers, golf is a means of relaxation—or it should be, if they keep their attitudes correct. For the professional, as stated above, it is a source of continued tension and pressure.

Even Kathy Whitworth admitted in 1973, "My nerves were completely shot. I shook so bad in the last tournament of the year I couldn't sign my scorecard. I knew then if I didn't back off I'd be out."

Many good golfers have found that getting away from golf for a period of rest and relaxation enables them to come back and play with a quiet mind. Bruce Lietzke even reverses it: He says he is a "serious fisherman" but a relaxed golfer. All the questionnaires about how golfers relax indicate that fishing is probably the most popular. Not only Lietzke but also Fuzzy Zoeller, Raymond Floyd, Ben Crenshaw, Tom Watson, Curtis Strange, Andy Bean, and many others follow fishing as their way to let down. Bobby Wadkins says that when he is in his fishing boat he is totally relaxed, far removed from the pressure of making the cut, bad lies, or three-putt greens.

Other golfers follow other pursuits. Hal Sutton is also a fisherman but his real love is riding and training cutting horses. Peter Thompson, who has won the British Open five times, likes to read political, economic, and social studies, and enjoys the theater and classical concerts.

Once again we find a close parallel between golf and life in general. We live in a culture that is characterized by stress, hurry, pressure, and strain. It has been aptly called the age of anxiety. Many are in vocations that produce stress and strain. From the time we were children we were taught to struggle, strive, excel, be number one. We are trained to strive; we are not trained to relax. Yet we all need some tension-reducing techniques that enable us to do our work better. As a wise man once said, "He who never lets go can't hang on."

Relaxation is an art, but it can be cultivated and is of great value, both on and off the golf course. It helps us to attain a quiet mind that will help us both work and play better.

[1]Edmund Jacobsen, *You Must Relax*. McGraw Hill, 1934, p. 51.
[2]*1974 PGA Book of Golf*. PGA Association, p. 32.
[3]For a full discussion of their findings, see Tom Nieport and Don Sauers, *Mind Over Golf*. Doubleday, 1968, pp. 12–13.
[4]Arnold Palmer, *My Game and Yours*. Simon and Schuster, 1963, p. 61.
[5]Bruce Devlin, *Play Like the Devil*. Doubleday, 1970, p. 110.
[6]Dorcas Susan Butt, *Psychology of Sport*. Van Nostrand, 1987, p. 202.

4

Their Concentration Was Specific and Expectant

One of the most frequent words appearing in the growing field of sports psychology is the word "concentration." It is true in all sports. There are no exceptions. Whether it is the basketball player at the free throw line, the wide receiver going out for a pass, the batter at the plate, the key to good performance is positive concentration. Skiers need it, cross country runners need it, an article in an outdoor magazine even insisted that bass fishermen need it.

Long before there was any such thing as sports psychology, Harry Vardon said, "In a majority of cases concentrated purpose is the secret of victory."

Henry Cotton, a fellow countryman of Vardon, said almost the same thing: "Concentration is the secret of scoring well." Apparently he knew how to score well. He won his first British Open at St. George's Sandwich, when he opened with rounds of 67 and 65. He also won two more and was recognized as the greatest British golfer since Vardon.

Cotton pointed out that the concentration of which he was speaking was not easily achieved. On the contrary, it could be very fatiguing, it consumed a lot of energy, and it could be hard work. He said he was often in good enough physical condition to play a good round without tiring at all, but that the concentration that was necessary was exhausting.

All good golfers practice concentration or they wouldn't have become good golfers. Joyce Wethered, whom we mentioned in the Preface, owed much of her success to her great power of concentration. Once, while playing for the championship of Britain, she was lining up a putt on the eighteenth green when a train went rattling by, just off the edge of the golf course. After the round some friends commented that it was too bad the train had to come along just at that time. "What train?" she asked. She was concentrating so hard she hadn't even heard it.

Tommy Bolt, in his book *The Hole Truth*, said that concentration is 75 percent of winning golf. He readily admitted that the swing is basic and all important, but once the swing is grooved, that is only 25 percent of the matter. "The rest," he said, "is concentration."[1]

There are two major kinds of concentration. One is intense, all consuming, uninterrupted. In the case of such players as Gary Player or Arnold Palmer, in their prime, it began long before they got to the golf course, even, in some cases, several days before the tournament began. This is not the kind of concentration that amateur or weekend golfers can, or should, attempt to acquire.

Wisdom of the World

People who are extraordinary in any field usually have the ability to slow down their mind enough to focus on what is in front of them. They can concentrate.[2]

Emery and Campbell

The other is intermittent concentration. This is characterized by such players as Lee Trevino and Fuzzy Zoeller. Trevino jokes with the crowd, talks to his caddie, and seems to be having a good time. But when he gets over the ball he immediately goes into real concentration. Fuzzy Zoeller is another who seems completely relaxed and at ease. He says he doesn't even try to concentrate for the four hours it takes to play a round of golf. That is too much effort.

No one ever concentrated as completely or as intensely as Ben Hogan. Sam Snead, who played with Hogan many times, said Hogan would say "Good luck" on the first tee and then go into his isolation booth and not come out until the round was over. George Fazio tells of being paired with Hogan when Hogan was in his prime. Fazio holed out a five-iron for a two. The crowd exploded. On the next tee Hogan pulled out his card to mark the score and said, "What did you have on that hole, George?" He was concentrating so completely on his own game he didn't even notice.

His caddie said Hogan instructed him not to say anything. He didn't want anything to interrupt his concentration. His caddie said on one occasion Hogan didn't even notice it was raining until he told him because his clubs were getting wet. Hogan himself said he sometimes concentrated so hard on a shot he almost felt like he had already hit it.

Wisdom of the World

Concentration is the ability never to look forward and never to look back.

Anonymous

If Hogan was the best at intensive concentration, Jack Nicklaus was probably the best at intermittent concentration. He apparently had great powers of concentration from the beginning. When he was only twenty, playing in the World Amateur Championship, he was bending over a four-foot putt when a gust of wind blew his cap off. He didn't change expression or position. He kept working on the putt and made it. In contrast to Palmer and Player, who began their concentration days before the tournament, Nicklaus says he can be discussing a business deal in the car on the way to the course, but when he puts on his spikes he can dismiss that totally from his mind and turn to golf. He also said in a magazine article that while walking down the fairway he can be discussing the size of a fish he caught until he begins to figure the yardage for the next shot—and then he goes into total concentration.

Good golfers practice to improve their concentration. Calvin Peete says that one of the reasons for his success is right here. He practices concentration as much as he practices his strokes. "The more you practice it, the better you get," he says. "If you can fully concentrate on a plan and the execution of each shot and block out distractions, you'll play better. If you let things bother you then you are in trouble."

A study of the world's great golfers, past and present, male and female, pro and amateur, reveals that some concentrated intensely, uninterrupted, through the entire round, some concentrated intermittently, turning it on and off as the occasion required—but they all had three things in common.

- Their concentration was always positive. (Negative concentration can do more harm than good.)
- Their concentration was always specific. (There is no such thing as concentration in general.) They concentrated on this shot, this putt, and nothing else.
- Their concentration was always in the present tense. (They shut out what happened on the last hole, or what might be necessary on the next hole.) Their concentration was always in the here and now.

In other words, concentration consists of two processes: "shutting out" and "focusing down." For the professional it means shutting out the crowd, the TV cameras, the size of the purse, anything that distracts, and focusing down on the shot at hand. For the amateur it means shutting out the sound of a lawn mower in the next fairway, the conversation of one's friends in the background, or the fact you are two down with only four holes to play.

Concentration is a great art. Concert pianists need it, surgeons need it, public speakers need it, scholars in the library need it. It is one great art that leads to maximum performance in any field. Positive, specific concentration enables one to play the game with a winning attitude and a quiet mind.

[1]Tommy Bolt, *The Hole Truth*. Lippincott, 1971.
[2]Gary Emery and James Campbell, *Rapid Relief from Emotional Distress*. Rawson Associates, 1986, p. 79.

They Played with a Quiet Confidence

Before the U.S. Open in 1971, Lee Trevino was being interviewed and was asked the usual question, "Who should be considered the favorite?" Jack Nicklaus was at the height of his career and was picked by most to be the winner. Trevino agreed. He said, "Nicklaus is the greatest player in the world. There is no one else like him." Then he paused a minute and added, "But I can beat him." That's confidence.

Before the British Open in 1981, Hale Irwin was asked by a reporter if there was a twelve-foot putt that had to be made to win a tournament, who would he prefer to have stroke it. Irwin instantly replied, "Me." That's confidence.

Ever since the game has been played, good golfers have been saying that the key ingredient in winning golf is confidence. Walter Hagen introduced a new element into the attitudes of winning golfers: almost complete and unlimited confidence. He had complete confidence that he could win. Henry Cotton said that confidence was the central factor in scoring well. Bobby Jones said that without confidence a golfer is little more than a hacker. More recently, golfers with such phenomenal records as Arnold Palmer and Jack Nicklaus agree that confidence is the most important single aspect in the mental or psychological side of golf. Bruce Crampton, who came to America from his native Australia to compete with the greatest golfers in the world, not only on the regular tour but now on the senior tour, said, "To be a winner you first have to have the confidence that you can win."

It is the key word in the lexicon of the sports psychologists. When such people as Dr. Bob Rotella, Gary Wiren, and others are consulted by some of the game's leading players, it is usually because they have lost their confidence or had their confidence shaken.

Wisdom of the World

*They can conquer who
believe they can.*
Ralph Waldo Emerson

All good golfers, past and present, agree that confidence is the one attitude that contributes most to winning golf. Yet in spite of the almost universal agreement on the value of confidence, no one knows for sure how to attain it, why a player has it one day and not the next, why some have it and others don't. This remains the great mystery.

The only way we know to answer some of these questions is to study the experiences of those who have demonstrated it in actual competition and see if there are any elements that are common to all confident golfers. The one thing that is very obvious is that confidence is not something they had from the beginning or that they had all the time. They were not born with it. They weren't always confident: not Bobby Jones, not Ben Hogan, not Byron Nelson, not Gary Player, not even Arnold Palmer or Jack Nicklaus.

Greg Norman came from Australia a few years ago and appeared to be the one that would take over the game. One year he came in second in all the major championships but the British Open—and he won that. The sky seemed to be the limit. Then he went into a slump. He missed a few cuts, he finished down in the pack in tournaments he had dominated the year before, his putting dropped off, he changed putters in an attempt to resolve the problem. In explaining it in an article in *Golf* magazine, he said, "Somewhere along the line I realized the problem wasn't the putter, it was the man wielding it. It wasn't my stroke, it was my confidence."[1]

When such great golfers as those mentioned above were not playing well, like Norman, they usually said that they did not have their confidence. When they played well they played with a quiet confidence. In studying their lives it seems that there were four things that they had in common.

1. First was a thorough knowledge of the game. Men like Nelson, Hogan, and more recently Nicklaus, Trevino, and Ballesteros know the basic fundamentals so well that they don't have to be concerned about them when they play. They can direct all their mental energies to planning the shot at hand. Their knowledge is so complete as to what is required in every situation that they just turn that over to the unconscious and focus entirely on the shot at hand—with confidence.

2. Good golfers gained confidence by practice—extensive practice. As Ben Hogan used to say at a tournament, "If you don't bring it with you, boys, you're not going to find it here." How Hogan practiced until he wore blisters on his hand is legendary. Henry Picard used to practice his irons from dawn to dusk. He became so confident of his approach shots that he once told a friend he felt each shot might go in the hole. Gary Player took Hogan for his model and would practice hours on end. He would go into a sand trap and not come out until he had holed three shots from the sand. Sometimes that took two or three hours, but he became the best bunker player on the tour. Stories are frequently told of seeing him practice eighteen-inch putts for long periods of time. When asked

why he practiced them since he never missed, he said, "The greatest thing for putting is confidence. And the greatest things for confidence is watching the ball go in the hole. I'll stand here until my confidence is high. The subconscious is watching the ball go in the hole."

Jack Grout, who taught Jack Nicklaus how to play golf, was interviewed by Nicklaus at the end of his instruction tape. Grout said that Nicklaus would practice for hours, in the heat, in the rain, in the snow. He even built a shelter with a stove in it so he could hit golf balls out into the snow though they couldn't find them until the spring thaw.

These men weren't just hitting golf balls when they practiced. Each session had a purpose. They studied their games. They reviewed their rounds. They were aware of their weaknesses and their strengths, and practiced their weaknesses until they became strengths. There may have been some good golfers who gained confidence without practice but we don't know about them.

3. The greatest single contributor to confidence is experience. Good golfers know they can play well because they have played well. We referred previously to Arnold Palmer's statement, "I never saw a hole I couldn't birdie." That's confidence, but the only reason he could say that was because he had birdied so many holes. Tom Watson had a shaky start on tour. He lost some tournaments he could have won. The reason was probably a lack of confidence, but when he did win then he won so often he became golfer of the year four times. Jack Nicklaus said that his primary asset was his high level of confidence, or, as Nicklaus put it, he "believes in himself." Watson himself said he knows he can play well because he has played well.

As we pointed out earlier, most players like Jones, Hogan, Nelson, and others had to gain their confidence the hard way, over a period of time. The one possible exception would be Nicklaus. He had so much natural talent, he had such excellent instruction while very young and such early exposure to competition, that he was a winner from the start. He won his first tournament when he was thirteen. When he was sixteen he won the Ohio State Open and qualified for the U.S. Open. When he was nineteen he played on the Walker Cup team in Scotland. When only twenty he made the lowest score ever recorded by an amateur in the U.S. Open; the next year he turned pro and won it. When he started on tour the game was dominated by Palmer, Casper, and other very experienced players. Nicklaus respected them but was never overawed by them. He had experienced success so young that he had a quiet confidence from the beginning.

As sportscasters are reporting the final round of a tournament and assessing the chances of the various contenders, they use an overworked phrase, "He has been there before"—by which they mean that his previous experience of winning has given him a bit of an edge.

Experience alone is not enough. Those who play well are those who have profited by experience. A man once boasted that he had thirty years of experience. A friend commented that he hadn't had thirty years of experience, he had one year of experience and had it thirty times. Good golfers have learned from experience. They have profited from their losses as much as from their wins.

4. If there is anything more important than experience, it is a golfer's mental attitudes—the way the golfer sees herself. Good golfers see themselves as winners. They expect to make good shots and hole difficult putts. All sports psychologists agree that confidence comes from confident thinking. A player first has to think confidently in order to play confidently. Lee Trevino says, "I drive straighter than anybody, so the more trouble there is, the better I like it." Dave Stockton entered the final round of the 1971 PGA with a one-stroke lead and Arnold Palmer in second place. When Stockton was asked how he felt, he said, "Nobody can putt and chip better than I can...I feel like I am going to win." The next day he scrambled in and out of bunkers, out of the woods, even out of the water, but he chipped and putted better than anybody and won his first major.

In the 1978 Masters, Gary Player, then in his forties, started the last day nine strokes back but he played a phenomenal round and won. In the post-tournament interview he was asked when he felt he had a chance to win. He said, "When I teed off."

Such statements as these were not based on conceit or wishful thinking. They were expressions of genuine confidence based on a thorough knowledge of the fundamentals, hours and hours on the practice tee, usually years of experience, and positive, confident mental attitudes. Such a concentration of effort and attitudes enabled them to play with a quiet mind.

[1]*Golf*, November, 1987, p. 188.

They Had Realistic Expectations

One year on a golfing tour of Scotland and England we were playing Royal Birkdale, the site of several British Opens, when we were lucky enough to have a caddie who had had long experience. He had carried for the British Open, for the Walker Cup, and for thousands of amateurs just like us. We asked him what was the biggest problem he had had in his long experience. He said it was carrying for people who expected to hit every shot perfect and then getting all upset when they didn't.

This is true not only of golf but of all experiences. In counseling I frequently hear people say, "Of course I am a perfectionist." The minute that statement is made, I know that person has set himself up for frustration. We want people to strive for excellence, we want people to improve, to try to attain their maximum performance, but perfection is not an option. No one has ever lived in a perfect town, been a perfect parent, had a perfect job, or played a perfect round of golf.

The great golfers didn't expect to. Jack Nicklaus himself said, "Even at my best, I've rarely hit more than six or seven shots in a tournament round exactly as I've planned and visualized them."[1]

Ben Hogan is recognized as one of the greatest shot makers of all time, but in his book *Five Lessons* he made a similar statement. He said he had played golf a long time, even had won several tournaments, before he knew before a round whether he might shoot a good score or a bad one. He said it was not until he realized that he didn't have to do a lot of things perfectly but only had to groove a few fundamentals that he began to play with confidence.

The classic illustration is Walter Hagen's most familiar statement. It is probably quoted as frequently as any other quotation in the history of golf. Hagen said that he knew when he left the clubhouse he would hit at least seven bad shots so when he hit one it didn't bother him; it was just one of the seven. Fuzzy Zoeller in more recent days echoed the same thought as Hagen. He said he knew he wasn't a machine, therefore he wasn't surprised at some bad shots and didn't let them upset him. They didn't expect perfection.

Wisdom of the World

We all need "the courage of imperfection."
Alfred Adler,
psychiatrist

Wisdom of the Fairways

You can't be a perfectionist and play golf.
Bob Toski

Peter Jacobsen said that when he came out on the tour, he had the idealistic notion that the superstars didn't hit anything but good shots. He said he had to learn that "the likes of Jack Nicklaus, Tom Watson, and Ray Floyd didn't hit every drive down the middle and every green in regulation. They don't," Jacobsen says, "and what's more they don't expect to." Jacobsen said that when he realized this, it came somewhat as a surprise to him and helped him understand some of the great players' effectiveness. "Their approach to mistakes allows them to play with a relatively free mind, unencumbered by pride or whatever."[2]

The great golfers have usually recognized their own humanity. They know that it is human to make mistakes, to hit bad shots, to miss short putts. There is another quote from Hagen which is not so familiar as the one above but is equally important. "I believe the majority of golfers expect too much in holing out," Hagen said. "There is no tragedy in missing a putt, no matter how short. We have all erred in this respect. Short putts are missed because it is not physically possible to make the little ball travel over uncertain ground for three or four feet with any degree of regularity. The mental side will overcome the physical side if we worry about a missed putt. It is far better that we count missed putts as part of the game and leave our minds free and open to make one without the suggestion entering the head that our putting stroke is all wrong." [3]

Julius Boros, who shared Hagen's philosophy, was playing in the PGA in San Antonio. He missed a putt of about twelve inches on national TV. He said, "One putt doesn't make a tournament," went on, and won.

Even the best golfers hit a bad shot, or have a bad round once in a while. In the 1961 Masters, Arnold Palmer needed a four on the last hole to win, a bogey five to tie. He hit a good drive with only one hundred fifty yards left to the green. It looked like a cinch. A careless seven-iron landed in the sand. Too clean a shot out of the sand sailed clear over the green. An average chip and a missed putt resulted in a six and a tie for second. Such stories could be multiplied for page after page and would include such names as Snead, Nicklaus, Trevino, Watson, and hundreds of others.

John Jacobs, the well-known teaching pro from England, distinguishes between what he calls "playing" and "competing." He says too many golfers try for perfection and then get discouraged when they hit some bad shots. A competitor, however, will bear down, even when he is not hitting the ball well, and will often turn a bad round into a good one.

Good golfers, even great golfers, not only hit bad shots; they also have bad rounds. If you want to check this out for yourself, pick any good pro on one of the tours and follow her from week to week in the paper for a period of six weeks or more. You will find that she has good days and bad days. She may win a tournament one week and not make the cut the next. This happens over and over again. No one wins all the time. Dick Aultman made a study of the day-to-day scores of the players in the four majors: Masters, U.S. Open, British Open, and PGA. The average maximum difference from one day to the next was 5.69 strokes.[4] Golf is the only professional sport where winning 10 percent of the time makes you the best in the world.

The moral is obvious. If the best golfers in the world hit some bad shots and have some bad rounds, why should the amateurs be surprised or discouraged when it happens to them? As stated above, this does not mean they should not try to improve. They should; that's half the fun. Everyone should strive for excellence, in golf and in life. Everyone should strive to reach his or her full potential. That is what the game is all about. More important than winning is to know you have played your best. That is the fascination of the game. It just means one should have realistic expectations—and perfection is not one of them.

The great golfers went to great efforts to improve their games. They had high standards and lofty goals. They did all they could to attain them—but they did not expect perfection. To expect perfection is to set oneself up for frustration. To accept imperfection is to play with a quiet mind.

[1]*Golf Digest*, June, 1985, p. 16.
[2]*Golf*, January, 1985, p. 98.
[3]Rick Aultman and Ken Bowden, *The Methods of the Golf Masters*. Coward, McCann and Geoghegan, 1975, p. 28.
[4]*Golf Digest*, November, 1987, p. 108.

7

They Enjoyed the Challenge of Competition

John Jacobs, to whom we referred earlier—the successful tournament player and teacher in England—distinguishes between "playing" and "competing."

It is estimated that there are more than 17 million golfers in the United States alone. Most of them are players. Only a few of them know how to compete. Competitors pay attention to the little things that give them a winning edge. One of the simplest is to arrive at the golf course in time to warm up properly. In all sports, a warm-up period is considered necessary for good performance. Basketball players run warm-up drills and shoot free throws. Baseball players take infield practice and hit from the batting cage. Football players do calisthenics and run plays. Even a church softball team will warm up before a game. Only amateur golfers attempt to hit their first shots with no previous preparation—but not the good ones. They warm up first by hitting full shots and spending a few minutes on the putting green. If there is one thing the average golfer can learn from the competitors, it is to be sure there is time to warm up.

In one sense, all the other things that are discussed in other sections of this study are an aid to competing: disciplined practice, relaxation, concentration, course planning—all of these help a person in competitive situations.

Another thing that competitors usually do is follow the same pre-shot routine every time, no matter what. When Julius Boros was winning major championships, he followed the exact same routine on every shot, especially on crucial putts. He would line up the same way, take his stance the same way, take the same number of practice swings on the 72nd tee that he did four days before on the first tee. It is said that Billy Casper was so meticulous about following the same pre-shot routine that if he was interrupted for some reason, he would put the club back in the bag and start all over again.

Good golfers leave nothing to chance. They know exactly how far it is to the green from almost any spot on the course. More than this, they know how far it is to the flag, and whether it is cut in the front of the green, the middle, or the back. They also know how far they can hit each club so they can make a choice and clear their minds of that whole issue. Then all they have to do is hit the shot.

Good competitors take bad bounces, bad breaks, missed putts, and occasional set backs for granted. They don't get upset by them. They expect them. They see them as part of the game. Walter Hagen almost enjoyed them. When he would find himself in a bad situation, he would wink at the gallery and say, "Now watch this one."

Good golfers slow down the pace when in competition. Julius Boros said that whenever he was in contention, he deliberately tried to slow everything down. This enabled him to avoid a fast, jerky backswing.

Bobby Locke, four-time winner of the Brisith Open, intentionally conditioned himself to play slowly. Gary Player, who often played with Locke, said if Locke were dying of thirst he would reach out slowly for a glass of water.

Gary Player followed his fellow countryman's example. In fact, Player took the matter of pace so seriously that he began to set his pace several days before a tournament. When he won the U.S. Open at St. Louis, he said he practiced pace for a whole week before the tournament by doing things more slowly than he was used to. He was careful to talk slowly, eat slowly, dress slowly, drive to and from the course slowly.

Bruce Devlin, when he came to America from his native Australia, said that one of the first things he had to learn was to slow everything down. He had played fast as an amateur in Australia but he soon found that wouldn't work on the pro tour. He said he had to learn to slow down, especially when tension built up.

Good competitors remain calm and collected when distractions occur. Distractions come in many forms, shapes, and sizes. It may be a partner's slow play, a shout from the crowd, a click of a camera, a bee buzzing in one's ear, the sound of a lawn mower or a chain saw in the distance, the weather—anything. Good competitors ignore these distractions.

Bobby Jones at one time in his career was noted for his outbursts of temper. He developed the capacity to ignore distractions to such an amazing degree that it did not effect either his game or his manners. Playing in the British Open at St. Annes in 1926, he was tied for the lead at the eleventh hole. He approached his ball and was set for the shot when a cameraman stepped out in front to snap his picture. Jones stepped back then resumed his stance but the cameraman did it again. This time the crowd literally pulled him out of the way. Jones pitched to the green and made his par.

We were following Lee Trevino at the Colonial in Fort Worth. He was playing the seventeenth fairway when a helicopter landed on the adjoining fairway just a few yards away. The crowd and the marshalls all rushed to see who and what it was. Trevino waited until they shut down the motor then drilled his shot to the green. The marshalls were more distracted than he was.

Good competitors never give up on a round. There are many instances where a golfer has begun with a poor start but by determination, patience, and persistence has turned a poor round into a good one. In the1971 PGA, Nicklaus began playing very poorly for him. He was very determined however, and by keeping on, and by one-putting eight of the last ten greens, he saved a 69 which could easily have been a 75 or a 76.

Bob Goalby once almost gave up on a whole tournament. He was playing in the Sahara International in Las Vegas. He opened with a 71 and 75 and figured 146 wasn't good enough to make the cut. He packed his bag, went to the airport, even got on the plane. Then he thought maybe the bumpy greens and strong wind had affected other golfers too. He went back to the course, found out he was still eligible for the final rounds, played well, and came in second—and won a nice check.

Johnny Miller describes an experience he had early in his career. He was leading the Masters on the final day when he began to think about the results. He said he was thinking about what he would say in his acceptance speech. He even wondered how he would look in the green jacket. It broke his concentration and he lost on the final holes. Good competitors don't put pressure on themselves by thinking of the purse, the media, the glory. They do not think of the results—only of individual shots. We recognize that in one sense this is expecting the impossible. Yet, to the degree that they are able to dismiss the results from their minds, the better they are able to perform the tasks at hand.

Winning golfers usually enjoy competition. Bill Campbell had one of the best amateur records in recent years. He competed in thirty-seven amateur championships and won the U.S. Amateur in 1964. He was interviewed by *Golf Digest* magazine some years later. Among other things, he said, "I believe deeply what a wise man once said, 'It is better to travel hopefully than to arrive.' In golf I have arrived on a few occasions, although in most cases I have been beaten along the way. But it is in the competition that the real fun exists."[1]

Fuzzy Zoeller, speaking of choking, said he loves it. He just wants to get in the kind of competition that brings pressure. Hubert Green also says he enjoys it: "He relishes the uneasy feeling of competition: sleepless nights, trouble eating breakfast, butterflies on the first tee."[2] "We all choke," says Curtis Strange, "You're not human if you haven't. We get just as nervous as the average guy playing for the club championship. It's relative. We learn how to handle fear better on this level, but sometimes we don't. There's not a player out here who hasn't choked."[3]

The classic quote came from Tom Watson the year that he and Jack Nicklaus had their famous duel on the final round of the British Open at Turnberry. They were all alone in the lead, tied going into the final holes. Watson turned to Nicklaus and said, "This is what it's all about, isn't it?" *Golf Digest* reports a foursome that say that they play for a dollar a hole. When asked if that wasn't pretty steep they said, "It doesn't matter; we never pay off." They were then asked, "Then why don't you play for five dollars a hole?" They said, "We couldn't stand the pressure."

How does one become a good competitor? Bob Toski says there is only one way: by competing. He calls it "composure by exposure." He says there is only one way to become a competitor and that is by testing yourself time and again in competitive situations. That is true—good golfers learned to compete by competing. That is only a partial truth, however. A lot of golfers have put themselves in competitive situations and did not become winning golfers. The ones who did became good competitors by applying the little things mentioned above that gave them a winning edge, and by developing those attitudes that enabled them to be at their best when they really wanted to play well. Knowing how to compete enabled them to play with a quiet mind.

[1]*Golf Digest*, May, 1982, p. 52.
[2]*Golf*, January, 1987, p. 100.
[3]*Golf*, January, 1987, p. 102.

8

They Kept Things as Simple as Possible

Golf is a game of eighteen separate units. Good golfers have always played it one unit—or, in other words, one hole—at a time. They knew that it didn't make any difference what they did on the last hole, whether it was good or bad; they had to focus entirely on the present hole. They also knew it didn't make any difference what the next hole was, whether it was hard or easy; they had to play the present hole and play it well.

Actually they kept things even simpler than that. They not only played one hole at a time; they played one shot at a time. Hale Irwin was quoted in *Golf Digest*: "I try to isolate each shot during a round and handle it as a separate challenge. Golfers often think about what they did on past holes or what the outcome of a match will be. The idea is to keep your mind in the present tense, concentrating on the shot at hand." [1] In other words, they kept things simple. As Sam Snead once said, "You can't hit the next shot until you get to it."

They not only played one hole at a time and one shot at a time; they permitted only one thought at a time. Actually it takes about a second to swing a golf club, and a person cannot think of more than one thought in that span of time. The good golfers don't even try.

They all try to avoid what Ernest Jones, the great golf teacher, called "paralysis by analysis." There are two kinds of thoughts in golf. One is used on the practice tee. There, analysis is good. That's what they are there for. These have to do with mechanics, swing, techniques, etc.; the focus is on the areas that need improvement. The others are play thoughts. These have more to do with results; they are kept simple, and minimal.

Tom Kite says he only tries to think of one swing thought during a round. He may change it from round to round but one thought is all he attempts. Never two. Many others have said the same thing. Gary Player says he has two thoughts. One is to get his weight to the left side. The other varies from round to round. When Tom Weiskopf was playing his best, he said he only thought of the word "tempo."

Byron Nelson, in his instruction book, pointed out that Bobby Jones used to say that if he was thinking about three things during his swing, he played poorly. If he was thinking of two things, he could shoot par. But if he only thought of one thing, he could win the tournament.

There is an old jingle that says,

> The centipede was happy quite
> Until a frog in fun
> Said, pray which leg comes after which

Wisdom of the World

Our business is not to see what lies dimly at a distance but to do what lies clearly at hand.
Thomas Carlyle

Wisdom of the Fairways

Think simply about your swing and you will have a simple, uncomplicated swing.
Peter Thompson

> This left his mind in such a pitch
> He lay distracted in the ditch
> Considering how to run.

On this there is almost universal agreement by the better golfers. The golf swing should be an automatic movement, which is difficult to do if the mind is cluttered with too many thoughts or ideas, like the thoughts they have on the practice tee. When they get on the course, they just turn it over to what some call the unconscious and others call muscle memory. Most sports psychologists advise that all thoughts on the golf course should be "target" thoughts. Good golfers, they say, focus on the target, not how to get it there. They focus on the target and then just let it happen.

The majority of good golfers keep things simple. They play one hole at a time, they make one shot at a time, they permit one thought at a time. This keeps the mind uncluttered so that they can swing freely and smoothly with a confident attitude and a quiet mind.

[1]*Golf Digest*, September, 1921, p. 54.

They Let Winning Take Care of Itself

Jim Flick, of the Nicklaus Flick Golf School, met for a day with the golf team of Texas Christian University. I was permitted to sit in on their sessions. After a full day of observation and instruction, they had a seminar session in the evening. The one thing I remember that Flick said was, "You've got to learn how to lose before you will know how to win."

Good golfers have learned both lessons. In an interview after he won the Masters, Ben Crenshaw made a very significant statement. "You learn to accept defeat graciously in golf. Unlike other sports, the game itself is a constant opponent. It never stops. A golfer is fortunate to win a few times. We spend our whole lives trying to conquer something, and we lose a lot more than we win."

This has been true of even the greatest. Peter Aliss has chronicled on an interesting tape the careers of the greatest players in the game from the days of Vardon down through the careers of Walter Hagen, Bobby Jones, and Gene Sarazen. He included Hogan, Cotton, Snead, Nelson, de Vincezo, on

51

down to Palmer, Player, Nicklaus, Jacklin, Tevino, Watson, and Ballasteros. They were winners all. But none of them won all the time. They all knew "the agony of defeat."

Golf is unique in this regard. As we said previously, golf is the only professional sport where an athlete can win 10 percent of the time and be the best in the world. In the World Series or the Super Bowl, half the players are on the winning side and half on the losing. Not so in golf. In the U.S. Open, or the Masters, one player wins, one is the runner-up, and all the rest are also-rans. Even the runner-up has small consolation except for the check. As the saying goes, "No one remembers who came in second."

It is true that, in 1945, Byron Nelson won eighteen tournaments, eleven of them in a row, but that has only happened once in the long history of golf and will never be repeated. The only one that has even come close is Nancy Lopez when she won five in a row, but she played in many other tournaments when she didn't win. If a golfer wins two or three tournaments in a year, that is considered news and is likely to get him, or her, voted golfer of the year. In professional golf one has to know how to lose as well as how to win, and it is a valuable lesson for the weekend golfer as well.

We live in a culture that puts an extreme value on winning, even to the point of winning at any price. The idea of sport as a game—the joy of the challenge, the satisfaction of a sincere effort, whether or not one wins—has been lost. All too often, the emphasis is "win or else." The result has been a lot of sports scandals, hiring and firing of coaches, and a great deal of unfortunate and unnecessary emotional strain on athletes.

Dr. Wayne Dyer, a psychologist who has written several popular self-help books, comments on this obsession with winning. "Of course winning can be fun, and even more fun than losing," he says, "but if you need to win to prove yourself, you have lost all healthy perspective. You can surely look at winning as something terrific to achieve, but you should be even more certain that your essence as a person does not depend upon the achievement."[1] Good golfers have recognized this. It has frequently been pointed out that Jack

Nicklaus has won more major tournaments than anyone. What is not so frequently pointed out is that he has come in second or third more than anyone else. Some of these were tournaments he very much wanted to win. But he accepts both the wins and losses with equal humility and grace. Many times in post tournament interviews he has said, "Nobody tries to win more than I do, but if I play my best and lose, the sun still comes up tomorrow"—or words to that effect.

Wisdom of the World

An athlete should feel no threat if he or she does not win, for others will then have done better and for that the athlete appreciates and respects them.[2]

Dorcas Susan Butt

This "win-at-any-price" philosophy is illustrated by Leo Durocher's oft-quoted statement, "Nice guys finish last." Of course, he was referring to baseball. We doubt if it is true there, but it certainly isn't true of golf. It certainly wasn't true of the players Peter Aliss included in his tape—Jones, Nelson, Palmer, Player, Nicklaus, Trevino, Watson and others—all of whom finished first, and all of whom are nice guys.

Those who have been winning golfers have all recognized that winning demands a price. It requires hours, sometimes years, on the practice tee to perfect a swing that will stand up under pressure, plus an equal amount of time and discipline to develop the mental toughness, the powers of concentration, and the confidence that enable one to play well. When Bruce Crampton joined the senior tour after a few years away from golf, he even surprised himself by becoming the leading money winner. Speaking of this he said, "I'm extremely proud of that. It's rewarding when the amount of hours that I've spent practicing and the calluses that I've raised pay off. All the trials and tribulations one goes through…not too many people see it all come together as it has for me."

Paradoxical as it may sound, there is such a thing as trying too hard to win. Jack Renner is a case in point. He turned pro in 1976 when he was only twenty. In his second year he was fourteenth on the money list and was touted as one of the next big winners. Then he went into a slump until 1981 when he was back to eleventh. This was followed by another period of very unspectacular golf. He did some evaluating of his game and discovered that thirteen times he was in the top ten during a tournament but only ended up with four top-ten finishes. His own evaluation was, "I probably was so obsessed with winning that I would play my way out of golf tournaments." Then he concluded, "I'm not so sure you win by being obsessed by winning."

Kathy Whitworth has won more professional golf tournaments than anyone else in the history of professional golf. When she had a chance to win number eighty-five and surpass Sam Snead's record of tournaments won, the desire to win was almost overwhelming. Friends, the media, the public, were all wanting her to win. She said she finally came to grips with the fact she was trying too hard to win. Whether she won eighty-five tournaments or not was not all that important. Then she not only won eighty-five but several more as well.

Time included a story on Mike Reid, who was on the tour for eleven years before he won his first tournament. He was the first golfer to win a million dollars without winning a championship. He described his emotions during those eleven years and then summed it up in this way: Speaking of his wife, he said, "Both of us had to let go of wanting it so bad. We looked each other in the eye and said, 'It's all right if it doesn't happen.' You know it wasn't two weeks later that it did."[3]

Long before Jack Renner and Kathy Whitworth, Harry Vardon and Joyce Wethered were the two dominant figures in the world of golf. They were without question the best male and female golfers of their day. Both revolutionized the game with their smooth and very effective swings. They also had another thing in common: Neither of them concerned themselves too much with whether they were going to win or lose. They just played without too much concern about the results. Since they weren't concerned about winning or losing, they could play with a quiet mind.

Good golfers have attempted to prepare themselves to the best of their ability. They try every time out to play up to their full potential, and let winning take care of itself. They were modest in victory and gracious in defeat. If they did that, they were winners in the best sense of the term, no matter what the score.

[1]Wayne Dyer, *Pull Your Own Strings*. Avon, 1977, p. 105.
[2]Dorcas Susan Butt, *Psychology of Sport*. Van Nastrand, 1987, p. 180.
[3]*Time*, June 6, 1988, p. 79.

10

They Learned How to Control Their Emotions

When Ben Hogan received the Bob Jones Award for distinguished sportsmanship in golf, he said, "Golf is a game of emotions, but if you don't control them you can't play."

It is interesting that the award had the name of Bobby Jones on it. No one ever had a greater struggle to maintain self-control. Also, no one ever did it more successfully. But it wasn't easy. He set for himself almost impossible goals and became furiously angry when he did not attain them. His anger was always directed at himself, never at his opponents or the course. Once while playing in the British Open he took three shots to get out of a bunker. He tore up his score card and came back to America. His caddie, Luke Ross, said that when Jones would throw his clubs he would retrieve them slowly to give Jones a chance to calm down before he had to hit his next shot.

One reason for his amazing success as a golfer, and which enabled him to utilize his fantastic natural ability, was that he developed the capacity to control these emotions. He said that he remembered something that had been said about the great Harry Vardon. One of Vardon's greatest assets was the realization that no matter what happened there was only one thing he could do: keep hitting the ball. This he did. It took Jones a long time to attain such control, but he did it. One sports writer of that day commented, "He stands forever as the greatest encourager of the highly strung player who is bent on conquering himself."

There is a story that goes back to St. Andrews: A judge was trying a case in which one of the St. Andrews caddies was being sworn in as a witness. The judge, not sure of his educational background, said, "Do you know the nature of an oath?" The caddie replied, "Aye, sir, I've carried your clubs many a time."

I entitled this chapter, "They Learned How to Control Their Emotions," because that's what they had to do. They learned it, but it wasn't easy. Even Julius Boros of the smooth swing and even temperament admits he had to learn this lesson also. He said that when he was younger he threw a few clubs, even broke some, but he also realized it didn't help much and it was pretty expensive. Like Jones, he had to learn to control his temper and, like Jones, he began to play better golf when he did. One graphic illustration is the time he won his first major championship, the U.S. Open of 1952. He had a two-shot lead on the field when he found himself in a bunker on the twelfth hole. Boros is usually a great sand player but this time he left it in the sand. His second attempt went clear across the green. He took two putts for a double bogey and he saw his lead vanish in one hole. His comment later was, "I decided I still had a long way to go to get those two shots back if I kept hitting the ball instead of the ceiling."[1]

David Graham puts it simply: "Before you can control the ball, you have to control yourself."

Some never learned it. Who knows how many golfers, pro and amateur, have limited their golfing careers because they couldn't control their tempers?

Tommy Bolt is the classic example. He was a man of great talent but his temper tantrums were legendary. They led to nicknames such as "Thunder Bolt." He was known to throw a club or two. There is a story—obviously apocryphal—that in one tournament they came to the eighteenth fairway and Bolt asked his caddie how far it was to the green. "It's 120 yards, Mr. Bolt," the caddie answered, and handed him a two-iron. Bolt said, "It's only 120 yards. Why did you give me a two-iron?" "Because it's the only club we've got left," the caddie replied. Those who knew him in his prime said he might have really been one of the great ones, had he controlled his emotions better.

The experts all agree: Losing control of one's emotions not only affects coordination, which destroys the swing, but also impairs judgment. John Jacobs says that everyone gets into difficult situations on the golf course. This is inevitable. What happens then depends on what Jacobs calls "mental equilibrium." Some golfers get so angry when they find themselves in trouble that they cannot think clearly. They try to pull off a miracle shot, which isn't very likely in golf.[2] The cause of stress is different for different people. I know from the days I taught graduate students that they had different levels of stress. A final exam could challenge some students to do well; others would panic. Some would become so filled with tension that they couldn't write. The same is true of golf.

Arnold Palmer, in his autobiography *Go for Broke*, speaks of the emotional nature of golf. "The golfer, good or bad, exists in an environment of constant turmoil—a turmoil within himself. We all know how a bad shot plunges many a golfer into such depths of disgust and self-recrimination that

---

Wisdom of the World

Self reverence, self knowledge, self control, these three alone lead to sovereign power.
Alfred Lord Tennyson

Wisdom of the Fairways

Ball control, course control, self control, these are the secrets of good golf.
Several golfing professionals

it destroys his next shot or his entire game. Or how a good shot will lift him to such heights of exultation that, carried away by his excitement, he'll go on to flub his next two or three shots."[3]

Jim Colbert, speaking as a tour player, says the real struggle in tournament golf is with oneself. He says that sooner or later you have to learn that you don't have to beat Nicklaus, Miller, or Player. The person you really have to conquer is yourself. That is your toughest opponent. [6]

The testimony of the experts is that golf is a game of the emotions. To control one's emotions is one of the greatest victories in life, on or off the golf course.

To bring this down to date, in the 1988 Byron Nelson Classic, Bruce Lietzke was leading the tournament on the last day when he bogeyed number eight and dropped out of the lead. This was very discouraging since he hadn't won in a long time. He said at that point he thought of Don January. He said he had observed January a lot and noticed that he never does anything fast, never gets flustered. He never gets flustered or mad at anything. Lietzke birdied the next hole and went on to win the tournament.

Wisdom of the World

Anger blurs your vision, misdirects your attention, depletes your psychic energy, breeds other painful emotions and destroys cooperation.[4]

Emery and Campbell

Wisdom of the Fairways

Don't let yourself get too excited by your good shots or too discouraged by your bad ones. You have to stay on an even keel to play your best. If you get to feeling down you're likely to get impatient and lose interest. If you get too excited you won't be able to think clearly.[5]

Sam Snead

In the 1988 Masters, Sandy Lyle was leading the tournament on the last day, but he three-putted eleven, hit his tee shot in the water on twelve and double-bogeyed that hole, and went into a fairway bunker on eighteen. It looked like he had blown his chances. Mark Calcavecchia was already in and a bogey by Lyle would give him his first Masters; a par would mean a play-off. All who saw it on TV know what happened. Lyle hit a seven-iron out of the trap, one-putted for a birdie, and won.

Afterward, Calcavecchia said, "He's 99 percent unflappable. All great players have the ability to handle ups and downs. I don't think I've ever seen him get mad." That's playing with a quiet mind.

[1] Julius Boros, *How to Play with an Effortless Swing*. Prentice Hall, 1964, p. 21.

[2] John Jacobs, *Practical Golf*. Quadrangle Books, 1972, p. 99.

[3] Palmer, *Go for Broke*. Bantam Books, 1973, p. 147.

[4] Gary Emery and James Campbell, *Rapid Relief from Emotional Stress*. Rawson Associates, 1986, p. 118.

[5] Sam Snead, *Golf Digest*, February, 1988, p. 52.

[6] *Golf*, April, 1975, p. 118.

11

They Played with Their Minds as Well as Their Clubs

Peter Aliss, in his videotape recounting the historical development of golf, made an interesting comment. He said golf is half archery and half chess. The good archers are the good shot makers who can drill the ball to the target. The chess players are the thinkers who demonstrate good strategy—what Ben Hogan calls management. This chapter is about the chess players, or the thinkers of golf.

It is frequently said that golf is a thinking person's game. After Tom Watson won the Open at Pebble Beach, he said that he won it as much with his mind as with his clubs.

Jack Nicklaus is frequently quoted as saying that golf is two different games. One is the physical game that consists of ball striking, learning the fundamentals, etc. The other is the mental game that consists of strategy, course management, tactics, and planning.

On one of those rare occasions when Hogan was a spectator at a tournament, he was asked to comment on the players and the influence their swing had on their standing. He said that a good swing gave a person a 25 percent advantage; the rest is management.

Most experienced professionals would agree with Hogan's statement. The year that Bruce Lietzke won at Colonial, he was interviewed by the Fort Worth Star Telegram after the tournament. He said, among other things, "You can go to the practice tee at any tour tournament and see pretty and perfect swings and most of them aren't making a cent. On the other hand I wouldn't classify the swings of Jack Nicklaus and Lee Trevino among the top ten. They win because they think better than anybody else on the golf course."

Raymond Floyd made a similar statement at the PGA in 1982. Floyd was having a good year. He said the reason he was playing better was that he was thinking better. He said that when he was younger he would always go for the pin, no matter what, and it often cost him strokes. This year he said he was taking into consideration what he could do and what he couldn't. He was careful to determine when he should take a chance and when he should play conservatively, especially when under pressure. He said the same thing about Nicklaus that Lietzke did. He said that the thing that separated Nicklaus "from the rest of us was that he's smarter. He always knows what he can do and can't do."

In evaluating the careers of the great golfers of the past and observing the better contemporary golfers, they all were good at archery, but the winning golfers were also good chess players. They thought through their shots. There are certain general principles of management or strategy that seem to be common to them all.

The truth of the matter is that management or strategy in golf is really not all that complicated. We can boil the strategy of golf down to a few often repeated statements.

> "Keep the ball in play."
> "Have a plan for each shot."
> "Play away from trouble."
> "Play for position."
> "Make wise decisions."
> "Play the golf course, not your opponent."

The first five statements can almost be summarized in the initial one: *Keep the ball in play.* These five words sum up the basic principles followed by most good golfers. From the tee they want to use the club and select the landing area that will keep the ball in play. When they do get into trouble, their first consideration is to get the ball back in play. Julius Boros, who did so well on difficult courses, such as those set up for the U.S. Open, said this was his primary objective: to keep the ball in play and go for pars.

This is the reason they *had a plan* for each shot, each hole, even each round. They never hit a "wish" shot; they never played a hole carelessly or thoughtlessly. Tom Watson says he has a game plan for each round, which means he has a plan for each hole, and he seldom varies from it. Billy Casper says a person should exert his energy planning a shot instead of worrying about it. This begins on the first tee and continues for each shot that follows. We heard Bob Toski point out the fact that each hole has a strength and a weakness. There is a good way to play the hole and a dangerous or foolish way to play the hole. The good golfer knows her strengths and her weaknesses, then she matches her strengths against the hole's weaknesses. This takes planning. This would vary from day to day according to the weather, and from golfer to golfer according to his or her skill. Cary Middlecoff said that this is one of the reasons for the great success of Gary Player. He never hit a careless shot; each shot was struck with a definite goal or plan in mind.

All of the above statements are included in the principle, *play away from trouble*. One of the best ways to keep the ball in play is to have a plan that will keep the ball in play, and the best way to do that is to play away from trouble. Most of the strategy on a golf course is determined by the hazards. Golf courses are designed to present alternatives and force a player to think. Sometimes it seems golf architects are attempting to deceive you, to tempt you to take unnecessary risks. Jack Nicklaus said his play improved when he began to think like a golf architect. We conducted an informal survey among a group of amateur golfers who were good enough to compete at the college level. One question was, "Do you think like a golf architect?" Almost none said that they did. Good golfers can play with a "quiet mind" because they are aware of the hazards, they know why they are placed there, and they play away from trouble.

Another statement that includes most of the others is *always play for position*. This is what Lee Trevino calls "placement." He says it is far more important than distance. Good golfers play for position from the tee; they want to be in position for a good second shot. On the par-fives or long par-fours, they want a second shot that puts them in position to have a good approach to the green. This is where Ben Hogan was a genius. He was always in position. Tommy Armour, in his book *How to Play Your Best Golf All the Time*, said always "play the shot that makes the next shot easy."[1] It is true that golf can only be played one shot at a time. It is also true that each shot is linked to the next shot. The good golfers plan ahead, knowing the position they want to be in for making the next shot easy.

They made wise decisions. This statement has many ramifications. It means, as we quoted Raymond Floyd earlier, good golfers are aware both of what they can do and what they can't do, and make decisions accordingly. It means that they know when to gamble and when to play it safe. Part of this is a matter of temperament. Arnold Palmer was more likely to gamble than Billy Casper because that was Palmer's nature and it was not Casper's. Even so, Palmer claims he never really gambles on a shot. He says he thinks he can make a shot or he wouldn't attempt it. Most students of golf strategy advise that it is usually safer to play it safe. For example, they usually put it on a seven-to-ten basis. If they think they can make the shot seven times out of ten, they go ahead; the odds are with them. If they are not sure of that, then they feel it is better to play it safe.

Wisdom of the Fairways

Treat your opponent with all due respect as a nonentity.

Harry Vardon

The most significant decisions a player has to make on the golf course are club selections. This may be one of the most overlooked factors in scoring well. The good golfers know what they can do with each club and under all conditions. The first thing they take into account is the lie, then the terrain, then the weather. Then they make the selection of a club that will accomplish their purpose in the light of those conditions.

The final statement of golf strategy is the old familiar *play the golf course, not your opponent.*

Golf is the only game where the opposition cannot determine how you play. In baseball, football, and basketball, coaches design a game plan whose main purpose is to confuse the opposition and force them to play differently from the way they have planned. Not so in golf: It is the golfer and the golf course. An opponent may distract a golfer, but not unless the golfer lets him. He still can play his own game. Lee Trevino said, "You'll never catch me playing my opponent. I play the golf course." Bobby Jones said that even in match play it was wise to focus on the course and not your adversary. After all, he reasoned, "it's old man par and you," whether the play is match or medal. Cary Middlecoff summarized the thinking of the most successful golfers when he said, "If you play the course intelligently you don't need to worry about the opposition."[2] By using their heads, they played with a quiet mind.

[1]Tommy Armour, *How to Play Your Best Golf All the Time*. Simon and Schuster, 1953, p. 22.
[2]Cary Middlecoff, *Master Guide to Golf*. Prentice Hall, 1960, p. 106.

12

hey Played in the Zone—
Sometimes

The ultimate of playing with a "quiet mind" is to attain what some golfers call "playing in the zone." Others call it "playing in a trance," some call it "being on automatic pilot," some call it "playing out of the mind." Whatever it is called, it is a unique and wonderful experience that does not occur except on rare occasions. That is why the title of this chapter includes the word "sometimes."

One of the really historic events in the history of golf in America was in the United States Open of 1913. Harry Vardon and Ted Ray, the two predominant players in England, were entered, and it was naturally assumed that one of them would win. Francis Oimet, a young ex-caddie who was relatively unknown, was playing, using a ten-year-old caddie. It was headline news when Oimet tied them and defeated them in a play-off. This was the first step in shifting the dominance of golf from the British Isles to the United States.

Oimet admitted that he was nervous on the first tee but his ten-year-old caddie told him just to keep his eyes on the

69

ball, and he managed to make a good drive and to sink a difficult putt for a par. This tied his illustrious opponents. After that he said "I seemed to go into a coma."

Other golfers have described similar experiences. Tom Watson calls it the "twilight zone." He says, "In my case I feel an inner calm. I'm nervous but nothing bothers me."

When Johnny Miller was having such a string of marvelous tournaments a few years ago, he was interviewed by a newspaper reporter who quoted him as saying, "When I get it going it's like I'm in a trance. I know what's going on around me, but I can block out everything. It's like I'm hypnotized. I can see the things that are going to happen. Everything is 'Go.' It's all green lights. I feel like I can birdie every hole."

He had that feeling when he shot a final-round 63 to win the Open in 1973. "That's the only round in my whole career when I felt like maybe someone upstairs intervened. I wasn't playing terrifically well and then, all of a sudden, I'm perfect. It was like someone was helping me and I was just going along for the ride. It's never happened like that since and it may never again."

Hale Irwin also uses the term "trance" to describe such experiences. He says when he is in, or near, the lead, "I get so immersed in the situation that I block out everything else. I get into another little world—a trance if you wish. I try to keep my mind specifically on what I'm doing. I don't allow it to wander much."

When Nancy Lopez won her second LPGA championship, she said after the final round, "When I started today, it seemed as if nothing was going to get in my way....It was like I was by myself, I didn't hear anything....Nothing else was there, just that little white ball and me. The feeling was there. I could tell it was there." She said she had the same feeling early in her career when she was doing so well.

When Nancy Little shot a final-round 64 to win the Dinah Shore, she said she was definitely in the "ozone," as she put it. "To tell you the truth I didn't know what I was shooting."

Gary Player also says he has had similar experiences. He says he has played rounds when he didn't know his score. He said he had had rounds when he hardly knew where he was. "I've also been in a don't-know-who-I-am sort of daze—total relaxation and complete control."[1]

None of these players claims to have this experience all the time, not even frequently. Tony Jacklin, winner of both the British and U.S. Opens, says he has experienced it a few times. When he was interviewed by the *London Sunday Times*, he said such feelings are difficult to describe. In fact, he said, you really can't explain them to someone who has never experienced them. Besides, he added, he didn't like to talk about them because they were too personal.

This is not an experience that is limited to golf. Other athletes speak of them as well. Tennis players also speak of playing in the zone when all of their shots are true and accurate. A pitcher may get into such a state of rhythm and concentration that he feels he can't be hit. A quarterback may get such a level of confidence that he feels he can't miss a receiver. When Michael Jackson scored sixty-three points against the Boston Celtics in an NBA play-off game, he said he was concentrating so completely on his play he wasn't aware either of the score or the game clock.

This is what Dr. Maslow, the great psychologist, called "peak experiences." Artists have them. Public speakers have them when they feel they are at one with their audience. Composers have them: Mozart said that sometimes his symphonies came to him all at once in their totality. The biographies of religious leaders commonly speak of moments of religious insight and understanding. In fact, this may be as akin to a spiritual experience as one can experience in sport.

Andy Bean, who is noted for his interest in literature and things outside of golf, commented in an article in *Golf Digest* that he had read that "a lot of artists try not to think of anything when they paint. They just like to do it and they do it. That," he said, "is the way one should play this game." In fact, he went on to point out that, in one sense, golf is an art form, and whenever a golfer gets in the "zone," or in "a trance," or in "a world of his own," then Bean contends he is an artist in the truest sense of the word.[2] We would agree.

On such days, or in such moments, the golfer is experiencing what is often called "maximum performance." In reflecting on those who claim such experiences, I found there are some things they all seem to have in common. They all had mastered the mechanics or the fundamentals. No matter how heightened a state of consciousness, it will not correct a bad grip. Most of them had had much experience before this happened. Oimet may be the exception, but most of them had been playing for a long time before such things occurred. While they had mastered the fundamentals, they were not conscious of them when such days occurred. Dr. David Burns, the psychiatrist, advises for more effective living to focus on "process rather than outcomes."[3] Dr. Coop, an educational psychologist who conducts a column in *Golf Illustrated*, uses almost the same terms. "Focus on process" he says, "rather than outcomes."

Peak performances do not come by analysis or by trying harder. They come when players are able to combine the mechanical, the mental, and the emotional to such a thorough extent that all blend into one complete experience and they just let it happen. Then they are playing with a quiet mind.

[1]Player, *Positive Golf*. McGraw Hill, p. 17.
[2]*Golf Digest*, December, 1984.
[3]David Burns, *Feeling Good*. William Morrow, 1980, p. 312.

First Conversation with Roland Harper

Dr. Charles Kemp: About fifteen years ago I wrote a book about the psychology of golf called *Smart Golf*. Byron Nelson read the manuscript and endorsed it. Such established players as Hal Sutton, George Burns, and Bruce Crampton spoke well of it. The only criticism I received was from amateurs who said it applied more to professionals than to weekend golfers. I think they were right—I don't want to make that mistake again. That's why I have asked you to share in this project.

As you know, the main body of this material uses quotes and illustrations from great golfers, men and women, past and present. This is the way it had to be. They are the only ones I can quote. What I want to do is make their experiences applicable to average, weekend golfers. After all, they make up the bulk of the twenty million people who play golf in this country.

In the thirty-eight years you have been teaching golf, you have probably taught as many amateurs as anybody. Let's begin our conversation right there. How many golfers do you suppose you have taught?

Roland Harper: I don't know. I never thought about it. I teach about one thousand lessons a year—probably between fifteen thousand and twenty thousand.

Kemp: That ought to be enough to give you some insight into the psyche of the average golfer.

Harper: That's right. I certainly hope so.

Kemp: As you know, the main body of this material deals with the mental and emotional side of the game. How important do you feel that really is?

Harper: That's what the game is all about.

Kemp: Why?

Harper: Because the mechanics are simple enough. That's not hard to teach or to learn, but when you talk about the mental side you have to deal with the emotions. You can't have highs and lows and expect to compete. That's not easy to teach or to learn.

If we could forget what we did in the past we probably could do pretty well, but we remember our bad shots, we hope we won't hit them again, and so it goes. On the other hand, when we are hitting the ball well, it tends to breed good shots.

Kemp: After I had evaluated all these records and illustrations of great golfers, I chose as my title, *They Played with a Quiet Mind*.

Harper: That's a super title. That's what it's all about.

Kemp: Can amateurs attain it?

Harper: Yes, a lot of them do. It pretty much depends on why they play. If they play it as a game, they can. If they try to make it a business, work for which they don't get paid, if they play to prove something to themselves or others, they will get frustrated.

Kemp: As the host pro for the Southwestern Bell Colonial National Invitation Tournament, you have had the opportunity to know and observe the best golfers in the country. Which golfers, in your opinion, had the best mental attitude?

Harper: Yes, I've known not only the best in the country but the best in the world. All the good golfers from all over the world have played here. Actually, by the time they get to this level, they are all about equal. But if I have to name three, it would be Hogan, Nicklaus, and Watson. They seem to be the best—and I underline the word *seem* because you don't know what attitudes are going on inside. Most of the guys who play here have good mental attitudes. That's how they got here. That's what separates them from the crowd, from people their age. These guys have anger and temper tantrums too, but not for long or they wouldn't be out here very long. Crenshaw, for example, gets a little angry now and then but it doesn't last. It's there and then it's gone and he is playing good golf again.

Kemp: The illustrations I have used in this material have been from men and women for whom golf was their career. It was the way they made their living. For most people that you teach, golf is not a vocation but a means of recreation. Do you think they experience the same feelings and frustrations that a professional experiences?

Harper: Yes, the only difference is in the degree. All golfers get frustrated, disappointed, discouraged at some time or other. The amateur has other outlets. He has his job, his career, etc., to take his time and to give him satisfaction. For the professional it is everything, he has more at stake, it is his living. But basically I think the emotions are about the same.

Kemp: Do you think the mental or emotional side of golf can be taught?

Harper: I think it can be taught all right, but I think it is more a matter of making people aware of it's importance. When I grew up I heard that the game was more mental than physical, but I really didn't understand what it meant.

There are so many facets to the mental game. Take a simple example. A guy can hit hundreds of seven-irons in practice and hit them well. Then he comes to a hole like seventeen at the TPC course. It is a seven-iron all right, but the green is completely surrounded by water. That makes his whole attitude completely different. He has to adjust to a different situation with the seven-iron in his hand than he is used to.

Kemp: I'm not asking you to be a psychologist but, as a golf pro, do you think a person can learn to change her attitudes?

Harper: Oh yes, I do, if the emotional problems are not too severe. It may take a lot of work for it is not easy to do. It is not like changing your grip. If the emotional problems are very deep—real anger, for example—it may take the skill of someone other than a golf pro.

Kemp: If the emotions are so important, why don't more people recognize it?

Harper: Are you talking about teachers or players?

Kemp: Well, both.

Harper: Teachers that are good instructors recognize its importance, but they don't know how to teach it. They know how to teach what to do with the hands, the arms, the legs, so they teach what they know. They don't try to teach what they don't know how to teach.

Kemp: What about players?

Harper: A good number of them are aware of it. They talk about it but they don't know what to do about it. They can't understand why they can hit a super shot one time and turn right around and hit the worst shot of their life. It's not that they don't know the importance of attitudes, etc., it's that they don't know how to control them.

Kemp: What emotions are the most common?

Harper: For men—anger. For women—embarrassment.

Kemp: How many people come to you and say, "I need some help with my attitudes"?

Harper: Not any.

Kemp: Why?

Harper: They think in terms of mechanics. If they have a bad hook or a bad slice, that's why they don't score better. They think if they hit the ball better, their attitudes will change. The fact is if their attitudes would change, they might hit the ball better.

Kemp: What does it mean to say that "Golf is a thinking person's game"?

Harper: We've already discussed that. The most important thing about thinking is that the thoughts must be positive. When you are set up over the ball, you have to think of a good shot. If you had a bad shot on the last hole and remember that, then you tend to tinker with your swing and pretty soon it is all confusion.

Kemp: Gary Player says, "What you think is the most determining thing you do on the golf course." Isn't that an exaggeration?

Harper: Not at all. It may be an understatement.

Kemp: Would you care to elaborate?

Harper: It all goes back to the other questions. You've got to be positive. You will miss some, sure—everyone does— but you still have to think positively. If so, you will play better.

Kemp: This word "positive" keeps coming up. I think everyone agrees that you have to think positively. What about negative thinking?

Harper: It is your downfall. That really is the problem. You can say it two ways. You should think positively or you should avoid thinking negatively—it's all the same thing. And it is not easy.

Take a simple illustration. Pitching. A fellow has a wedge shot to the green. He hits it too far. The next hole he has a similar shot. He thinks, "I don't want to do that again." So he dumps it on the edge of the green way short. Why? Because he's thinking negatively. He's thinking, "Don't go too far," when he should be thinking, "Get it close."

Qualities of Character of Those Who Played with a Quiet Mind

Section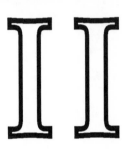

Golf is a test, not so much of the muscle, or even of the brain and nerves of a man, as it is a test of his innermost veritable self; of his soul and spirit; of his whole character and disposition; of his temperament; of his habit of mind; of the entire content of his mental and moral nature as handed down to him by unnumbered multitudes of ancestors.

Arnold Haultain
(on the walls of the World Golf Hall of Fame, Pinehurst)

1

Perspective:
They Had a True Sense of Value

Wise men tell us that one of the major tasks in life is to maintain a sense of values, to keep things in their proper perspective. Perspective is defined by the dictionary as "the capacity to view things in their true relation and relative importance."

Why golfers find this so difficult to do is what Arnold Haultain calls "the mystery of golf." In the first paragraph of his book by that name he asks, "Will someone tell us wherein lies the extraordinary fascination of golf?"[1]

The mystique is so real, the fascination and the challenge are both so frustrating, that all too many golfers, both pro and amateur, sometimes have difficulty in keeping golf in perspective or in seeing it in terms of its true relation and relative importance.

There are those who have done so. Francis Oimet, who brought stature to American golf when he defeated Harry Vardon for the U.S. Open in 1913, said, "To win a major championship is a great personal satisfaction, but after all it is only another game of golf."

Jack Nicklaus has personified this perspective as much as anyone. He has made many statements following major tournaments that underline this whole idea. Consider a few. After he lost the British Open in 1975 by one stroke, a tournament he very much wanted to win, he said, "Really it's just a game." In a magazine article in 1976, he said, "Golf's been a big and important part of my life, but there's more to life than chasing a little white ball around."[2] After he lost the Doral by one stroke he said in the post tournament interview, "Sure I wanted to win very badly, but let's remember it's only a game, and let's keep it that way." This attitude of keeping it just a game may be one secret of his long career. In an article in 1985, he said, "I try to give it my absolute best every time I tee it up, but when it doesn't work out I put it out of my mind and look forward to the next time. After all, the sun will still rise the next morning, however hot I may have been when it went down."[3]

Not many would disagree with such a position, although, in the heat of competition, it is easy to forget. The desire to win, the desire to play well, is so strong for most golfers that it is all too easy to let a loss in a tournament or a match, or just a bad round, get all out of perspective.

Betsy King, who was selected LPGA player of the year in 1984 when she had three wins and twenty-one top-ten finishes, said, "I have my game in perspective. I practice, have a more positive attitude and don't live or die on the golf course."

Wisdom of the World

Keeping our values straight is the biggest challenge we face each day.

Theology professor

Wisdom of the Fairways

Hey, pick up your head and smile a little bit. It's just a game called golf. It's not as important as a lot of things.

Hubert Green

The experts point out that keeping things in perspective also helps one play better. Johnny Miller, speaking of pressure putts, advises, "Remind yourself that your life does not depend on whether you make or miss a short putt, that golf is not the be-all and end-all of your existence. These thoughts can depressurize your mind and bring you down to an efficient performance level so that you'll be able to handle the putt more calmly."[4]

Byron Nelson, in his most recent book, said essentially the same thing. "If you'll convince yourself that the next crucial shot you have to hit is not the most important thing you'll ever have to do, you'll be much more relaxed and able to execute the shot."[5]

What Miller and Nelson are saying is keep the game in perspective, see it in terms of its true relation and relative importance.

There is a mystery about golf. It is a fascinating game, a great game, for many people the greatest game there is—but it is a game and should be seen in that way. If the experts are correct, when a golfer does keep it in its true perspective then she will both play better and enjoy it more. Then the golfer will see it in its true relation and relative importance and be able to play with a "quiet mind."

[1]Arnold Haultain, *The Mystery of Golf.* Applewood Books, 1908, 1988, p. 1.
[2]*Golf Digest*, April, 1976, p. 50.
[3]*Golf Digest*, February, 1985, p. 58.
[4]*Golf*, September, 1987, p. 37.
[5]Byron Nelson, *Shape Your Swing the Modern Way.* Golf Digest Books, 1976, p. 121.

2

Dedication:
They Were Dedicated Persons

    Great golfers were all dedicated to the pursuit of excellence. Otherwise they wouldn't have been great golfers. We mentioned earlier a tape by Peter Aliss entitled "The Golden Greats of Golf," in which he traces the development of the golf swing from the time of Harry Vardon and James Braid to Tom Watson and Steve Ballesteros. As one watches the high moments in the careers of Walter Hagen, Bobby Jones, Gene Sarazen, Henry Cotton, Peter Thompson, and many others, one is impressed by the fact that they dressed differently, played with different equipment, had different swings, but they all had two things in common: They all looked the same at the moment of impact, and they all were dedicated persons.

    Some years ago, when Nick Seitz interviewed Ben Hogan for an article in *Golf Digest*, he asked Mr. Hogan if he thought there would ever again be one man who dominated the game. Hogan replied that there might be, but he paused and said, "He'll have to be an awfully dedicated man."[1]

No one is a better example of this than Mr. Hogan himself. Grantland Rice, who knew them all in his day, said Hogan was the most dedicated golfer he ever encountered. Jimmy Demaret, who knew Hogan as well as anyone, said, "Sure he has great skills with the clubs. So have many fine golfers. But none can surpass his determination to win; his quiet confidence that he will win...his complete concentration, and his long and continuing hours of practice. We're all serious about golf, make no mistake about that, but Ben has a single-mindedness of purpose that makes the rest of us look like carefree school boys."

Gary Player, who took Hogan as his model, worked as hard as any golfer who ever played, with the possible exception of Hogan himself. When he was still a young golfer he knew he would have to work harder than anyone else because of his size and weight. They said his swing was too flat and that he was not long enough to reach the par-fives at Augusta. No one predicted an outstanding future for young Gary Player.

When he came to America he found that what they said was true. He couldn't reach the par-fives at Augusta. He went back to South Africa and hired his own trainer to work on his strength. The numerous stories about his dedicated practice sessions sound like exaggerations, but they are true. As I said earlier, he would go into a sand trap determined that he would not come out until he had holed out three shots if it took him all day, and on occasion it did. Needless to say, he became the best sand player in the world and not only won

---

Wisdom of the World

Take what you want and pay for it.
Old Spanish proverb

Wisdom of the Fairways

Dedication comes from wanting something badly enough that you discipline yourself to work hard enough to make it happen.[2]
Jack Nicklaus

but won tournaments on more continents than any golfer up to that time.

A dedicated approach to the game has been a characteristic of all the world's great golfers. Player says he smiles when people tell him how natural his swing appears. They don't realize the hours and hours of practice he committed himself to before it appeared natural. Sam Snead is reported to have the most natural swing in golf. He says he spent many hours before it became natural. Lee Trevino says he hit thousands and thousands of balls before he became effective. The list could go on and on. No one demonstrated this more than Henry Cotton. Scott and Cousins, in their book *Golf's Immortals*, said that before Cotton came into prominence winning his three British Open titles, he would hit thousands of balls in practice, often going without lunch, and then in the evening he would go out to the garage and hit more balls into a net. He said he had practiced putting so much that it was easier to bend over than to stand up straight. In the words of Scott and Cousins, "There never has been a more dedicated golfer than Cotton. His thirst for practice and his hunger for knowledge of the game which he was determined to master were the keys which opened the door to his success."[3]

A more recent example is Calvin Peete. He is recognized as one of the straightest drivers on the tour, one of the most

---

Wisdom of the World

If I stop practicing one day I can tell the difference.
If I stop practicing two days my family can tell the difference.
If I stop practicing three days the public can tell the difference.

Paderewski
the great pianist

Wisdom of the Fairways

Every day you don't play or practice is one more day before you get good.

Ben Hogan

consistent players in recent years. He has won the Vardon trophy, he won over a million dollars in three years, he has won the tournament players championships against the best players in the game. What seems so remarkable about all this is that he had so many odds against him. Ben Hogan and Gary Player began practicing in their childhood. Peete never swung a club until he was twenty-one. Furthermore, he fell out of a tree when he was twelve and broke his left arm. It healed permanently crooked. While other present-day tour players were playing college golf with good coaches or working on their games under expert guidance at country clubs, Peete, the son of a migrant farm worker, was peddling odds and ends out of the back of his car. When he read in the paper how much Jack Nicklaus was making playing golf, he thought it was worth a try. He went back to Florida and began practicing all day and into the night. When it was too dark to practice by daylight he would go to a baseball diamond and wait until the game was over and then practice until the lights were turned off.

His amazing consistency and rapid success didn't come easily. It was hard work. He says, "There aren't any short cuts to golf....I've been on the practice tee until I couldn't close my fists." Only complete dedication made Calvin Peete the player that he is.

Dedication is one of the qualities of excellence in almost every field. Great artists had it, great scientists had it, great statesmen had it—and great golfers had it. They were so dedicated to improvement, to attaining their full potential— they practiced so hard and so long—that when it came time to play they could play with a quiet mind because they knew what they could do.

Obviously the above paragraph applies to high-level golfers, whether they are pro or amateur. What golf means to an individual, only each individual can answer for herself. For the casual golfer, who plays primarily conversational golf and just wants the fun of an occasional outing, there is no need to go into such terms as dedication or commitment. There is nothing wrong with that. Golf is a great game for an occasional day out of doors with one's friends. That is fine. But the person who really wants to improve should remember what Calvin Peete says: "There are no short cuts" to excellence in golf. It takes dedication, time, and effort. But it is through the dedication of time and effort that one is finally able to play with a quiet mind.

[1]*Golf Digest*, September, 1970, p. 33.
[2]*Golf Digest*, April, 1976, p. 50.
[3]Tom Scott and Geoffrey Cousins, *Golf's Immortals*. Hart Publishing Co., 1969, p. 113.

3

Responsibility, Humility, Patience: They Were Persons of Character

Thomas Boswell, in an article on winning major championships, said, "It takes character to win a major championship." It takes character to win anything at golf. Someone once said, "Sports don't build character, they reveal it." We don't know who said that for the first time. We have seen it attributed to more than one person. We hope it isn't entirely true. We think sports can also help develop character. The second part of the statement is certainly true: Sports do reveal character, none more clearly than golf.

We pointed out in another section that most golfers are persons of integrity. They play by the rules, even to the extent of calling penalties on themselves. They also observe the courtesies, but there are other qualities of character necessary for good golf.

I heard Davis Love II, an instructor at the *Golf Digest* schools, make a statement that intrigued me. He said, "Golf appeals to persons who can accept responsibility." I had never thought of it in those terms, but the more one ponders it, the more one realizes that it is true, especially in comparison with other sports. In football, a player only plays on offense or defense or the special teams. In baseball, a player plays one position and usually only one. What happens in another part of the field is another player's responsibility. Some even play only if a right hander is on the mound, or a left hander. In basketball, each player plays both offense and defense but if he tires, or has an off game, the coach either rests him or replaces him as the case may be.

If it is to be
It is up to me.
                                        Anonymous

Perhaps it is because
you, and you alone, are
to blame if you miss it,
that you feel so keenly,
so intensely, a fumbled
stroke—another proof of
the uniqueness of the
game.[1]
                                        Arnold Haultain

None of the above is true in golf. The golfer plays all the positions (hits all the clubs herself). There is no one to run interference for him, no relief golfer (hurler) to bail her out if she's having a bad day, no one to rest him for a few holes if he's tired. The golfer does it all.

The golfer serves as her own coach. There is no one to call the plays (shots) for him, no one to plan his strategy. The only help she is allowed to receive is from her caddie, which in some cases can be significant, but the fact remains the golfer must accept responsibility for her, or his, own play.

Another quality of character that is necessary for a golfer is humility. The game itself should keep one humble. Good golfers play with a great deal of confidence but very few boast about it. The classic example, here as in so many other cases, is Jack Nicklaus. Early in his career when he was only twenty-five years old, Ward Thomas of the *Manchester Guardian* observed Nicklaus' great skills as a young golfer and wrote, "There is in this admirable young man the stuff of the fantastic, the phenomenal, the likes of which may never be seen again." These words were written long before he had attained his unequaled record in major championships. Thomas wrote, "In all the time I have known him, I have seen no sign of vanity, neither have I heard him boast about his golf, his income, or anything else." Then he added, "Imagine how insufferable he might have been." Twenty or so major championships later, the description is still valid.[2]

Wisdom of the World

I believe the first test of a truly great man is his humility.

Ruskin

Wisdom of the Fairways

Golf is an umbling game.
Old Scottish saying

Of all the qualities of character necessary to be a good golfer none is more necessary than patience. Bobby Jones, who spent seven years of frustration and embarrassment and seven years of amazing success, said the only difference in the bad years and the good ones was patience. The swing, he said, was the same. He had learned to play with patience.

After Sandy Lyle won the 1988 Masters he said "Patience is my fifteenth club." He had had some ups and downs but he prevailed and won with his fifteenth club.

The final quality that we would mention is that overworked word "desire." Sam Snead once said, "Give me a player with a little bit of talent and a great amount of desire and I'll pick him every time over a guy with a great amount of talent and a little desire."

Tom Nieporte and Don Sauers made a study of the psychological aspects of fifty leading professionals. Their conclusion was, "The one psychological strength which all successful professional athletes seem to share is desire...the deep motivation to succeed which we call desire."[3]

Bruce Crampton—who did so well on the PGA tour, took a few years off, and came back to dominate the senior tour in

1986—said, "There's no secret to this sport. There's no one right way to do it. People I play with in pro-ams ask me all the time what's the secret to better golf and I say, 'There isn't any'....The ingredients for success are desire and determination and self discipline and fortitude, but there's not a secret formula for it."[4]

Jack Nicklaus put it simply. "Desire," he said, "is the most important factor in golf."[5]

The overall theme of this little volume is a "quiet mind." The contention is that one will play better if the mind is free from confusion and tension. One of the best ways to attain a quiet mind is through the development of qualities of character such as responsibility, humility, patience, and desire.

Wisdom of the World

*How poor are they that have not patience.
What wound did ever heal but by degrees?*
William Shakespeare

Wisdom of the Fairways

Old man par is a patient soul and he that would travel the long road with him must be patient too.
Bobby Jones

[1] Arnold Haultain, *The Mystery of Golf.* Applewood Books, 1908, 1988, p. 9.
[2] Herbert Warren Wind, ed., *The Realm of Sport.* Simon and Schuster, 1968, pp. 411f.
[3] Tom Nieporte and Don Sauer, *Mind Over Golf.* Doubleday, 1968, p. 12.
[4] *North Texas Golfer*, September, 1986.
5 Nicklaus, *Golf My Way.* Simon and Schuster, 1974, p. 255.

4

Integrity and Courtesy: They Were Honest, Thoughtful, and Fair

I was speaker at the banquet for the Texas-Oklahoma Junior Golf Tournament. An incident occurred in that tournament that beautifully illustrates what we have been saying here. An eleven-year-old boy by the name of Blake Ladd double-chipped when approaching a hole. No one saw it, but he called a two-stroke penalty on himself. He said the reason was, "I love this game too much not to be honest. Golf is like a friend and you need to be honest with your friends."

Dr. Richard Cabot, the great physician/philosopher, was also a sports fan. He once said, "To win easily is not much fun. To win by cheating leaves us aware that, in fact, we did not win at all."

Golf is a game of integrity. It is one of the few sports in which the participants serve as their own referees and scorekeepers. No other sport permits the contestants to keep their own scores, enforce their own rules, and call penalties on themselves. Can you imagine a halfback going down the sideline and telling the referee that he actually stepped out of bounds, or an outfielder saying to the umpire that he actually

95

trapped the ball, or a basketball player calling a foul on himself? Yet golfers call penalties on themselves all the time.

Dow Finsterwald had a chance to win the Masters. After he had holed out a putt he took a practice putt on the edge of the green—not an uncommon practice in everyday rounds, but illegal in tournament play. After the round he remembered and called a penalty on himself. Arnold Palmer, playing in the British Open at Royal Birkdale, noticed that his ball moved ever so slightly. He called a penalty on himself. Beth Daniels, playing in the U.S. Women's Open, was in a hazard on the eighth hole. As she addressed the ball, it moved. Without a moment's hesitation she called a penalty on herself. Tom Kite did the same thing in the Colgate World at Pinehurst. He lost by one stroke. These illustrations could go on indefinitely.

> ### Wisdom of the World
>
> *While we believe in no man's infallibility, it is restful to believe in one man's integrity.*
>
> Morely,
> speaking of Gladstone

> ### Wisdom of the Fairways
>
> *That's just the way the game is played.*
>
> Bobby Jones
> (after calling a penalty on himself because his ball moved—and being reminded that no one saw it)

Such incidents illustrate the truth of a statement by Herbert Warren Wind: "As we all appreciate more and more keenly, sport without sportsmanship is nothing."[1]

A few years ago, Doug Ford wrote a little book for beginners, *Getting Started in Golf.* He pointed out that playing by the rules is not only the nature of the game but that a person will play better if she observes them. He said that if a player does something that isn't allowed by the rules, he not only is taking advantage of the ones he is playing with, but he is also offending himself. He said when a player does something that is not allowed by the rules then that person will be playing with a disturbed mind. To quote him exactly, he said, "If you are considerate of your opponents and play by the rules, you will be playing with a *clear mind*...and be thinking golf."

The greater the person the greater the courtesy.
Alfred Lord Tennyson

In everything do to others as you would have them do to you.
Matthew 7:12
("The Golden Rule")

Golf is a game designed for gentlemen and ladies. Certain courtesies have evolved over the centuries. Most golfers observe them. Good golfers not only play honestly, they also play courteously.

Golf is one of the few games in which a player does not try to confuse, irritate, or take advantage of an opponent in any way. In almost any other sport such as baseball, basketball, or football, it is considered quite appropriate to attempt to distract, to disturb, or to upset the opposition. Not so in golf. There are occasional expressions of gamesmanship, but they are the exception. In the main the good golfers give their opponents every opportunity to perform at their best. This is the golden rule as applied to sport.

A common sight when Arnold Palmer was at the height of his popularity and followed by enthusiastic crowds was his quieting the gallery so his opponent would have every chance to perform free of distractions or disturbance from what the sportswriters called his "army." In the 1978 Masters, Larry Mize and Greg Norman were in a play-off. On the second extra hole Mize missed the green and ended up down a fairly steep bank. Norman was on the green with a long putt. Mize chipped a miraculous shot to the edge of the green, the ball rolled slowly down to the cup and dropped in. Of course the crowd exploded. Norman still had a putt to tie. It was Mize who was quieting the crowd so Norman would have a chance to make his putt without interference.

The attitudes of the players are reflected in the behavior of the crowds. At other professional sporting events, the crowds do all they can not only to lend support to their own team but to distract the opposition. This is quite generally accepted. In fact, TV commentators speak of how influential it is when the crowd "gets into the game." Players also speak of how it can influence the outcome of a game. In golf it is just the opposite. The crowd intentionally keeps out of the game. There are some unfortunate exceptions, such as at the 1978 Open at Shinnecock when some fans heckled Greg Norman, but these are rare. The usual practice is for the crowd to maintain complete silence. It may be the final and deciding green, the score may be tied and tension is at its height, but the crowd surrounding the eighteenth green is completely silent. The outcome will be determined by the skill and poise of the golfers, not by any other influence.

Courtesy is a delightful quality of character anywhere. It is especially so in golf. Those who play honestly and courteously are playing with a quiet mind.

[1]*Golf Journal*, May/June, 1938, p. 33.
[2]Doug Ford, *Getting Started in Golf*. Cornerstone Library, 1979, p. 116.

5

Perseverance: They Could Rise Above Disappointment

Ben Hogan said to me in a private conversation, "This game has many disappointments."

This has been true of the best of them. Two of the winningest golfers in history are Sam Snead and Jack Nicklaus. Sam Snead has won more tournaments than anyone except Kathy Whitworth, but he never won the Open. He came close several times. In 1939 all he needed was a par on the last hole; he took an eight. You know he was disappointed.

Even Nicklaus, with his amazing record, knew the meaning of disappointment. He said the most difficult experience he knew in golf was to lose a big tournament that he thought he had won. It was in 1972, he had already won the Masters and the U.S. Open, and he had a chance at the elusive Grand Slam when he went to play in the British Open at Muirfield. It was one of his favorite courses, and although he started slow, he caught the leaders on the last day at the sixteenth hole. He figured that one birdie and two pars would do it—not unrealistic for him. Instead he bogeyed sixteen, parred seventeen and eighteen, and saw Lee Trevino chip in from off the green to win it. Afterward he said, "I can't shake the feeling I had it right in my hands and let it get away. It was the toughest loss of my career."

Some have had to overcome discouragement and disappointment outside of golf that affected their play. The early black players such as Charlie Sifford and Lee Elder had to deal with racial prejudice and bigotry that was both unfair and unjust, but they did it and played good golf as well. Lee Trevino, Calvin Peete, and Chi Chi Rodriguez all came up from poverty before they became winners at golf. Fuzzy Zoeller, Lee Trevino, and Ken Venturi had physical difficulties that were very discouraging.

Much space could be spent on overcoming adversity outside of golf, but that would require a much bigger volume than this. Here we are interested in being disappointed or discouraged on the golf course—and, as Hogan said, this game has many disappointments. It ranges all the way from a bad bounce to a poor round to losing a tournament to a prolonged slump. All great golfers have experienced such disappointments; there are no exceptions. The rest of this chapter will list some of their experiences. We shall include only successful golfers so that it will be clear that this is common to all.

Wisdom of the World

Never, never, never give up.

Winston Churchill

Wisdom of the Fairways

They say you can tell a man's fiber by how speedily he recovers from a harsh set back.

Herbert Warren Wind

We mentioned Ben Hogan—he too knew disappointment. Of course there was the accident that kept him off the course for a year. Then when he returned it was only to play with great pain. But he did and won again. Perhaps the most disappointing experience he had was the year he thought he had won his fifth Open, something no one else had ever done. Gene Sarazen even announced on the air that he had won, but he didn't take into account a club pro who was still on the course. Everyone knows that story. Jack Fleck came in to tie and force a play-off the next day. Hogan's legs just wouldn't take him another eighteen holes.

Arnold Palmer thought he had won the Open in 1966. He was leading the field by seven strokes going into the last nine holes. What he was thinking about was beating Hogan's record. His closest competitor was Billy Casper, who admitted he was only trying to protect second place. Casper not only made up the seven strokes, he won the tournament. Disappointment.

There are some things that do not appear in the papers. Mac O'Grady, who won the Tournament of Champions in 1987, tried *seventeen times* in the qualifying school before he finally got his tour card. Keith Clearwater is another example. He failed the qualifying school test four times and knocked around the mini tour for a few discouraging years before he finally won at Colonial, his rookie year, by shooting two 64s the final two rounds.

These illustrations could go on and on. Ken Venturi led the Masters in 1956 while still an amateur. He was playing beautifully. The last day he shot an 80. John Mahaffey was in a position to win the Open in 1976 but was the victim of an unbelievable five-iron shot by

> **Wisdom of the World**
>
> *If you're going to have peaks you have to accept valleys.*
>
> Anonymous

> **Wisdom of the World**
>
> *If a developing athlete is to be successful, he or she must trade on his or her own abilities and, what is more important, must develop the psychological resistance necessary to accept losses and setbacks.*[1]
>
> Dorcas Susan Butt

Jerry Pate who nipped him at the finish. In 1979 Tom Watson was having a fantastic year. He had won more money than anyone in history up to that time. He had won several tournaments and had finished high in the ones he didn't win. He was the odds-on favorite to win the Open and publicly stated that that was his one goal and objective. He didn't make the cut. Disappointments all.

We could cite literally dozens of other examples. George Burns had a chance to win his first major in the 1981 Open at Merion. He had played very well, but David Graham had an unbelievable final round and won it. On the last green George was seen applauding with the gallery when Graham walked onto the green, a show of good sportsmanship and an acceptance of discouragement. All he could say was, "I didn't lose it, David won it."

In 1976 Greg Norman led all of the majors at the end of the third round but only won one, the British Open. All of the others were disappointments. Bob Tway was responsible for one of the disappointments when he holed out a sand shot on the last hole of the PGA. Tway had known disappointment too. He came out of Oklahoma State as an all-American. They said he couldn't miss, but he tried three times to get his tour card. Each time he came up short, so he went on the mini tour, he went to Asia and Europe, he worked on his game until at last he too became a winner.

Ben Crenshaw also came out of college with great promise. He won the first tournament that he entered. After that he was disappointed for a long time. Twice he was runner-up in the Masters. He lost the PGA in a play-off. He missed winning the Open by two shots. He was second twice in the British Open. All of these were real disappointments, but in 1984 he won the Masters on its fiftieth anniversary.

All of those mentioned above were great golfers. All were winners. All knew disappointment. What does all of this have to say to the average golfer?

1. This is the nature of the game. If we are going to play well, if we are to enjoy the game, we must accept this fact. Disappointment and discouragement are a part of the game.

Those who have played it well have accepted this fact. Dale McNamara was Nancy Lopez's coach at Tulsa University. He commented on her tenacity and courage. He said, "You've got to wake up in the morning, look in the mirror and say you're damn good, then go about your business. Nancy has a tough mental attitude without being tough."

2. This is not unique to golf. This is true in all walks of life. Read the lives of the great statesmen, the great artists, the great scholars, the great scientists: In almost every case they had to deal with disappointment and discouragement before they became successes in their fields.

3. Recognize that bad bounces, bad rounds, frustrations on the golf course, are disappointments—that is all. They are not catastrophes, they are not disasters. These are disappointments—real ones, to be sure—but nothing more.

4. Recognize that whether or not they become major emotional concerns is up to us. We have a choice. We can see them as disasters—we can play mind games such as "poor me" or "ain't it awful"—or we can recognize disappointments as a part of the game and take them in stride. The golfer has a choice.

5. See them as challenges. It takes more character to continue to give one's best on a discouraging day than it does to hit 250-yard drives or to sink a long putt. Facing disappointments in a positive spirit can help build character.

We have contended throughout these studies that to play with a quiet mind is a means both to playing well and to enjoying the game. One of the real tests is on those days when we are disappointed or discouraged. That is when the golfer needs to play with a quiet mind.

[1]Dorcas Susan Butt, *Psychology of Sport*, p. 168.

6

Imagination: They Could See with the Mind's Eye

Arnold Lazarus, noted psychotherapist, published a book entitled *In the Mind's Eye*. He devoted an entire volume to describing the practical values that can be attained through the use of regular, positive, mental imagery. It can improve personal relationships, reduce tension, increase self-esteem, have a healthy effect on both mind and body, but most important of all for our purposes, it can improve performance.

Horton Smith some years ago wrote an article entitled "Using Your Imagination in Your Golf Game." He pointed out that this is a part of the touring pros' ability that cannot be observed by the gallery, but it is there nonetheless. Furthermore, he said that this is a practice that anyone, pro or amateur, can develop and use to advantage.

Gary Wiren, a golf professional who holds a Ph.D. from the University of Oregon and has studied the mental side of golf extensively, wrote an article in *Golf Digest* in which he said, "Creating positive mental images is as important a part of scoring as creating club head speed. Good players see good results before they swing."[1]

That this is true is evident by the statements of some of the game's greatest players. Jack Nicklaus wrote, "I am not an especially introspective individual, yet by training, I developed a very lively imagination when it comes to selecting golf shots. I can 'see' all my options in my mind's eye during the process of choosing a shot. Once the choice is made, I then try to visualize the flight of the ball to the target even more vividly before I step up to it....Next I try with equal intensity to visualize the swing I need to make to execute the shot I have pictured. Only after these mental exercises do I step up to the ball."[2]

Wisdom of the World

In a contest between the imagination and the will, the imagination will win every time.
William James

Nicklaus calls this "going to the movies." Tommy Bolt uses the same analogy. He says you should see each shot just as if it were on a motion picture screen. "You see it just the way you want it to be played, then you simply carry it out with your actual swing."[3]

Wisdom of the Fairways

Disciplined imagination is the essence of championship golf.
Tom Weiskopf

In 1986, when Greg Norman was winning tournaments all over the world, including the British Open, he said he was visualizing the flight of the ball really well. As a result he felt he could shape the shot as he desired.

This power of the imagination is true in all areas of the game. First, the *driver*. In tour statistics Calvin Peete consistently is rated as the most accurate driver on the tour. He says he sees the trajectory of each drive in his "mind's eye" before he ever addresses the ball.

It is especially true of trouble shots. Hale Irwin has a great capacity to make shots from difficult situations, a skill that has enabled him to win three U.S. Opens. He once wrote, "You see professionals play some of their best shots when they're in trouble because they put aside their emotions and concentrate even more than normal, using imagination and creativity to fashion a shot that will put them in the best possible position for the next shot."[4]

It is equally true of the short game. Eddie Merrins, well-known teaching pro, wrote an article on the short game. He discussed all the traditional things; the grip, the stance, the stroke, etc., and then he said, "You have to design the shot in your mind that you think can best get you close to the hole." His concluding statement was, "A good tip on playing pitch and chip shots is to paint a mental picture of the shot before the execution, then when you select the club, it's just a matter of positive execution of the picture you have in mind."[5]

Of course it applies to *putting*. Mickey Wright, who has dominated the LPGA tour, said when she was putting well she could "envision the entire putt, including the ball falling into the cup." She would foresee the path the ball was going to take, the stroke she was going to have to make to get the ball started on that path, and finally, in her mind's eye, she would see the ball disappear in the cup.[6]

It even includes the *mental game*, although this is usually done before the golfer reaches the course. For years good golfers have reviewed their shots in their mind's eye and played the course in their imagination while at home or in a hotel room. This not only improved their ball-striking effectiveness but prepared them mentally for anticipated competition. The idea that one can improve one's skills while relaxing in an easy chair without even hitting golf balls seems a bit far fetched, almost too good to be true, but this has been validated by research many times.

This is not something new. Good athletes have been doing this for years. Horton Smith, whom we quoted earlier, describes an occasion when he was not feeling well and felt it was unwise to go out in the inclement weather. What he did was stay in his room and visualize each hole and the way he would play it. He finished in the money in four straight tournaments and never practiced at all. Gary Player followed the same procedure when he won the U.S. Open at Bellrive in

St. Louis. He paced off the course, studied the greens, then sat in his hotel room and played the course over and over in his imagination. When time for the tournament came, he felt confident because he had already played the holes and played them well. Raymond Floyd said he did the same thing the year he won the Open at Shinnecock Hills. Byron Nelson, in his book *Shape Your Swing the Modern Way*, says he has learned a lot just lying in bed visualizing his game. Johnny Miller admits he doesn't practice a lot, but he thinks about golf a lot. Sports psychologists advocate this all the time. Their books and articles are full of it. It applies in many areas. Abram Chasins, a concert pianist, says that mental practice is the most important of all forms of practice for a pianist.

This is true because, as Dr. Rotella says, "Our body learns and reacts similarly to both actual and imagined experiences."[7] If the advice sports psychologists give their clients is right, in the future, practicing in the imagination may be considered as important as practicing on the practice tee. It must be emphasized very strongly that if anyone wants to follow the example of such players as those cited above, the imagination must be regular, it must be frequent, and it must always be positive. Perhaps one of the greatest resources for playing with a "quiet mind" is to do so in the "mind's eye."

[1]*Golf Digest*, February, 1980, p. 73.
[2]*Golf Digest*, November, 1982, p. 68.
[3]Tommy Bolt, *The Whole Truth*. J. P. Lippincott, 1971, p. 54.
[4]*Golf Digest*, September, 1982, p. 38.
[5]*Golf and Club*, 1971, pp. 34f.
[6]*Golf Digest*, May, 1982, p. 105.
[7]Rotella, *Mind Mastering for Better Golf*. Prentice Hall, p. 32.

7

A Sense of Humor:
They Could Laugh at Themselves

The great enemy of the golf swing is tension. Everyone agrees on that. Golfers will try almost any means to reduce tension. Some advocate relaxation exercises, some hypnosis, some positive thinking, some deep breathing, some visualization and imagery: All sorts of things are suggested to reduce tension and gain that winning edge.

In none of the golfing literature is laughter suggested, yet a sense of humor is one of the greatest resources there is to reduce tension and anxiety. There is a new growing awareness of the power of humor to promote emotional, even physical, well-being. I have in my library a book entitled *A Handbook of Humor and Psychotherapy*, co-edited by William A. Fry, a clinical psychiatrist, and Waleed A. Salamach, a clinical and consulting psychologist. This is not a joke book. It is a book written for professionals in the mental health field. In its pages, sixteen different authors testify to the value of humor in enhancing mental and emotional health. This is but one of several such publications that speak of the relaxing and healing power of humor.

Does this mean a golfer should not take the game seriously? No, it means he should not take himself too seriously.

One of the great contributions of golf to life in general is a sense of humor. Golf was invented on the edge of the North Sea near St. Andrews, Scotland, on an October afternoon in the fifteenth century at ten o'clock in the morning. The first golf joke was told that afternoon about 3:15—and they have been telling them ever since.

The story is told, no doubt apocryphally, that when Harry Vardon was playing with an amateur in Scotland, the amateur kept losing balls in the Scottish rough. He finally ran out of balls and asked Vardon if he could borrow one to finish the round. Vardon replied, "Whatever would I be doing with another ball?"

Wisdom of the World

Humor is the capacity not to take ourselves too seriously.

Encyclopedia of
Mental Health

Wisdom of the Fairways

So what, my wife still loves me, we've got money in the bank and the dog won't bite me when I get home.

Cary Middlecoff

When Bobby Locke came to America from his native South Africa and began winning money from American pros, some were critical of him. They said his left hand grip was too strong on the club. Locke replied, "It's OK, you see, I take the checks with my right hand."

Golfers don't pretend to be comedians. If they did they probably wouldn't be good golfers, although Lee Trevino and Chi Chi Rodriguez come close.

The golf journals are full of "Trevinoisms." When he first won considerable money on the tour, he said he thought he would buy the Alamo and give it back to the Mexicans. He also said that up till now he had been a Mexican, but since he had all this money he thought he would be a Spaniard.

Trevino's humor is not the kind of the comedian who plans his jokes ahead. His is the spur of the moment humor that is a spontaneous reaction to the occasion. Once when he was warming up for a tournament, a woman in the gallery behind him was "oohing" and "aahing" after each shot. Trevino turned and said, "Look lady, I'm the U.S. Open champion. What did you expect, grounders?"

Once when Trevino was asked if there wasn't a lot of pressure when he was putting for first place worth thousands of dollars. He replied, "Heck no, that's someone else's money. Having a four-foot downhill putt for a ten-dollar bet when you've only got five dollars in your pocket—that's pressure."

Chi Chi Rodriguez is almost as good an entertainer as he is a golfer, and that's pretty good. Everyone who has seen him play laughs when he makes a long putt and turns his putter into an imaginary sword and wipes the blood from the blade with his handkerchief and returns it to its imaginary scabbard.

He carries on a continuing line of banter with his playing partners, the crowd, anyone who will listen. He will make such comments as, "I was such a little kid I got my start as a ball marker," or "The amateur's best wood is a pencil."

Commenting on Jack Nicklaus and his wide range of activities, Rodriguez said, "Nicklaus became a legend in his spare time." He once described a situation where he was on the green with a long putt by saying, "I was on the dance floor but so far away I couldn't hear the music." He said he asked his caddie how to play it and the caddie said, "Keep it low."

Trevino and Rodriguez are two of a kind but occasionally some of the other pros unwind enough to say something clever. Larry Zigler was playing in the U.S. Open, but not playing well. When he was moving from a green to the next tee, a spectator asked him how he was playing and he said, "Right-handed."

Jim Dent is noted for his long—but not always accurate—drives. He remarked, "Yes, I can airmail it all right, but I don't always get the right zip code on it." Ben Crenshaw, when experiencing a slump, said, "I went fishing and my first cast missed the lake." Sam Snead, when reminded that he had won tournaments in four different decades, said, "How much is a decade these days?" Jerry Barber told of a friend who came to the first tee and had an unplayable lie.

Peter Jacobsen was playing in the British Open in 1986 at Royal St. George's when a streaker broke through the crowd and dashed across the fairway with British police in hot pursuit. Jacobsen, who was playing that hole, dropped him with a tackle that would have been worthy of a defensive back in the NFL. When asked why he did it, he said, "He was in my line."

What the world needs is a sense of humor—a good laugh. The world is full of sad and unfortunate things. A bit of humor to brighten the day is a welcome respite. It won't solve the world's problems, but it can make life a little more enjoyable.

There are literally hundreds of golf jokes—whole books full of them. With all due respect to those who favor other sports, there are very few tennis jokes, or bowling jokes; golf alone has made a contribution to the world's store of humor. We should be grateful. Would that more players could have a few laughs while they play, or at least smile a little. It would be more fun, and it just might help them play with a quiet mind.

8

Serendipity:
They Enjoyed the Fringe Benefits

Grantland Rice, the great sports journalist, once said, "Golf is twenty percent mechanics and technique, the other eighty percent is philosophy, humor, tragedy, romance, melodrama, companionship, confidence, cussedness and conversation."[1]

Bobby Jones once made a similar statement. It is inscribed on a wall at the World Golf Hall of Fame at Pinehurst and reads, "The game as played on the golf course represents only a modest part of the pleasure, enjoyment, and satisfaction that come to a person because he is a golfer."

A book entitled *The Joy of Nature* speaks of the value of being aware of the beauty of the natural world: the trees, the hills and valleys, streams, and lakes. All of this is available on a golf course—and in some places a view of the mountains, in others the vast outreach of the sea. On all courses there are clouds overhead and grass under the feet.

Wiren, Coop, and Shean, in their book *The New Golf Mind*, contend that it would even improve one's game to be aware of the world of nature. "Contemplating nature is one of the most obvious pleasures in golf," they say. "Yet it is often overlooked, especially by those so committed to excellence and improvement that anything that does not directly relate to their own game passes them by. If some of these self-ordained Hogans gave in to a little casual bird watching between shots they'd probably play a lot better."[2]

As a matter of fact, Ben Crenshaw is an ornithologist and can identify birds in any part of the country where he may be playing. He said he began watching birds as a kid in Texas. He is occasionally noticed watching the trees instead of the fairway. He tells about the American gold finch he spotted at the Buick Open, or the scarlet tanager he saw soaring over the practice green at Muirfield Village, or the red hawk he saw during the 1985 PGA at Cherry Hills.[3]

There is healing power in nature which, in our modern world of concrete canyons and hurry and speed, we seldom experience. The poets and philosophers have always recognized this. When Emerson was a young man, worried and troubled about many things, a wise old aunt urged him to get out of doors and let the world of nature speak to him of larger things. He did and it helped. Where better to contemplate the world of nature than on a golf course?

> **Wisdom of the World**
>
> *Walk slowly my friend,*
> *you'll see more.*
>
> Scottish saying

Golf is an art, not a science. Arnold Palmer wrote, "What other people find in poetry or art museums, I find in the flight of a good drive—the white ball sailing up into the blue sky, growing smaller and smaller, almost taking off in orbit then suddenly reaching its apex, curving, falling, describing the perfect parabola of a good hit, and finally dropping to the turf to roll some more, the way I planned it."[4] A bit overly poetic perhaps, but golf is a poetic game.

If golf is an art, then a golf course is an art form. It is truly a work of art, the transmitter of a rich heritage that goes back for centuries. A modern golf course is not a new development. It is something that has evolved for hundreds of years, ever since those first shepherds on the edge of the North Sea by St. Andrews took their shepherd crooks and hit rocks at rabbit holes.

Jack Nicklaus said that one of the reasons for his success was "the appeal of the golf course itself....A golf course was simply a good place to be; a source of constant pleasure and contentment quite apart from the game itself."[5]

Those who find the greatest pleasure in an art museum are those who have the greatest appreciation of what constitutes a great painting. Those who appreciate a golf course are those who understand what makes a great golf course. A good golf course is fair. A good golf course is challenging but not intimidating. It provides variety. It requires all the shots. A good golf course requires decisions. It must be played intelligently if one is to score well.

Wisdom of the World

He who has a thousand friends has not a friend to spare but he who has an enemy will meet him everywhere.

Old Arabian proverb

Last but far from least of the "fringe" benefits of golf is the great privilege of friendship. We live in an impersonal society where people live in large cities, attend large universities, work in large corporations, vote in large political parties— where we have become serial numbers rather than persons and friendship is a lost art. Not so in golf.

There is a delightful little story of a child who went in to his mother and said, "Mother, I wish I was two little puppies so I could play together." He was stating a basic law of life that we want to have friends. In golf, we can "play together." Granted, golf is also competitive and in competition we play against each other, especially in professional golf, but we can still play "with" our opponents and we can still be friends.

The fringe benefits are one of the best parts of the game of golf. The beauty of nature, the aesthetic beauty of a well-designed golf course, the joys of companionship—if we can appreciate these things as we play with a quiet mind, they are present no matter what we score.

[1]*Golf Journal*, November/December, 1986, p. 15.
[2]Gary Wiren, Dick Coop, and Larry Shean, *The New Golf Mind*. Simon and Schuster, 1978, p. 59.
[3]*Golf*, January, 1987, p. 53.
[4]Palmer, *My Game and Yours*. Simon and Schuster, 1963, p. 10.
[5]Aultman and Bowden, *The Methods of Golf's Masters*, p. 180.

9

Enjoyment:
They Had a Good Time

Dr. Robert Rotella, the sports psychologist, wrote an article in *Golf Digest* entitled, "Have Fun and You'll Play Better." Among other things, he said, "Certainly there is a time to get serious and work. But there is also a time to relax and enjoy the fruits of your labor. Practice is work. Competing on the course is your reward. Have fun!" He quoted the great golfer from Australia, Peter Thompson, who has done so well in the British Open and on the senior tour, who said, "You think best when you're the happiest." And Rotella added, "I can't say whether that works in your business. I guarantee it does in golf."[1] Kathy Whitworth said she couldn't think of anything she'd like to do or enjoy so much as golf. No wonder she played so well.

Unfortunately, all too few golfers experience this. I recall very clearly a conversation I had with John Elliot of the *Golf Digest* Instruction Staff. We watched a foursome come up to the tee at a course in Florida. I commented, "They don't look very happy." John replied, "Let's face it, there aren't many happy golfers." I thought, "What a pity," but it's probably true.

117

There have been a few great golfers who proved that you can play good golf and have fun too. When the late Henry Cotton toured this country, he is quoted as saying, "It's a game and supposed to be fun—maybe not fair, but fun all the same."

Of course some mention would have to be made of Walter Hagen. Once when he was asked how to play in the wind, he said, "Keep swinging and keep smiling." Dick Aultman, in a sketch of Hagen's career, said that his view of life was, "So what if I lose today, life is still fun and I'll win sooner or later."[2]

Few have approached Hagen's capacity to enjoy a round of golf, but in more recent years Lee Trevino and Fuzzy Zoeller have come close. Trevino seems to be having fun whether he's warming up for a tournament or playing a practice round, whether he's leading a tournament with a chance to win or in danger of missing the cut. All golf fans who saw Fuzzy Zoeller in the U.S. Open waving a towel at Greg Norman in mock surrender were grateful for a person in a tight situation who could still look at the situation lightly. Actually, of course, he didn't surrender, but won the Open the next day in a play-off. Afterward he said, "If my win in the Open proved anything, I think it was this: Golf is a game, and you can have fun playing it."

No one would accuse Arnold Palmer or Jack Nicklaus of not being dedicated golfers or of being poor competitors. Palmer said in his book on putting, "It is a sin in my firm conviction to play golf and not enjoy it."[3]

One year (1984) when Nicklaus was not playing well, according to his standards, he said to himself, "You're not having fun with what you're doing...and above all, golf is supposed to be fun. As a kid you let it fly and then went and found it. Golf was always fun in those days. Either do that again or quit."[4]

When Johnny Miller was asked to speak to the golf team of his alma mater, BYU, he gave a lot of practical advice, such as "The key is how you sail through the waters of adversity," and "It's not how good your good shots are, but how bad your bad shots are." His final point was, "Golf is fun. Look at every shot you hit as a new experience and enjoy it. Every time you hit a ball, it's a new happening. Take time to look at a shot and enjoy the challenge involved. Then look at the finish, the result, and enjoy it."

Ben Hogan, who took the game as seriously as anyone who ever played, said that he found the most pleasure in practicing. He said he would rather practice than play because it was more fun. In an interview with Ken Venturi on CBS in 1989, he said, "There is no greater pleasure than improving." The idea that practice can be fun is a thought that many golfers should consider.

Regrettably, all too few golfers find pleasure in either play or practice. Granted, for the professionals it is big business and is the way they earn their living. Still they need to recognize that they have chosen a game as their means of livelihood, and a game by definition is something to be enjoyed. For the amateur, it is a form of recreation and recreation is also by definition something to be enjoyed. If Dr. Rotella is correct, a golfer, pro or amateur, will play better if she enjoys it, and if she really enjoys it she will be playing with a quiet mind.

Wisdom of the World

Most people are about as happy as they make up their minds to be.
Abraham Lincoln

Wisdom of the Fairways

What does it profit a man if he makes a 200-yard approach shot if he doesn't enjoy the game?
Tommy Armour

[1]*Golf Digest*, June, 1987, p. 162.
[2]Aultman and Bowden, *The Methods of Golf Masters*, p. 28.
[3]Palmer, *Complete Book of Putting*, p. 87.
[4]*Golf Digest*, September, 1988, p. 100.

10

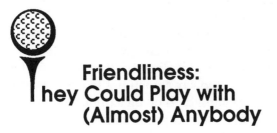

Friendliness:
They Could Play with
(Almost) Anybody

One of the most neglected areas of those who write about the mental side of golf is the influence that one's playing partners can have on one's attitudes and, in turn, on the score.

I am not talking about the oft-quoted statement of strategy, "Play the golf course, not your opponent." We have talked about that in another section on course management. That refers to the ability to shut out another person's score so that one plays his own game and concentrates on the golf course, not on what another player is doing. Here, we are not talking about another golfer's score but on the other player's personality. Letting another person cause one to get angry, frustrated, or irritated can do as much to destroy a quiet mind as anything we know.

Even the touring pros are not exempt. A few years ago Chi Chi Rodriguez liked to entertain the fans by running up and putting his straw hat over the hole when he made a long putt. The gallery liked it but the other pros weren't amused. In fact, they complained until Chi Chi discontinued this little act. A few years ago in the televised skins game, Tom Watson

121

was disturbed by some things Gary Player was doing and complained about it. Several pros on the senior tour were concerned by the way Bob Toski was marking his ball and complained to the point that Toski dropped off the tour for a while. He was not trying to cheat. He gave himself no real advantage, but some players were upset over it.

We're not talking about gamesmanship either. That is an intentional attempt to disrupt a golfer's concentration. Back in the days when most tournaments were match play, one of the old-time pros who was being defeated by a rookie would compliment him and say something to the effect that "You are so good, we should go on an exhibition tour together." The young player would get so excited about teaming up with a name pro that he would usually lose his concentration and his game would come apart. Walter Hagen used to concede short putts on the front nine and then when they got on the back nine, where it really counted, and his opponent had a short putt, Hagen would just look the other way. The fellow was usually surprised at first. He hadn't practiced any short putts all day and would usually miss.

While it is the exception, some amateurs sometimes resort to disrupting another player. I was playing in a little amateur tournament when one of the players would jingle the keys in his pocket while others were putting. One player was disturbed by it and said so. Fortunately, such things are rare.

Usually the distractions are unintentional. They come in many shapes and sizes. Sometimes it is simply because a player is playing his best. When Hal Sutton moved from the amateur ranks to the pro tour he found himself paired with Jack Nicklaus. He said, "Do you have any idea how intimidating you can be?" Now young pros are intimidated by Sutton. I was working with a young pro who was a rookie on the tour. He played very well in the early rounds of a tournament and found himself in second place and paired with Tom Weiskopf. Naturally there was a bigger crowd than he was used to—and the presence of Weiskopf himself. The young pro said, "Even my caddie was scared."

When an amateur is playing with someone who hits the ball a lot farther than she does or is scoring much better, there is a tendency to try to hit the ball too hard or to feel embarrassed.

There are many distractions and they can be divided into categories. There is the conversationalist. He loves to talk, sometimes even on one's backswing. He isn't out to play golf as much as to converse with his friends. Golf should be a friendly game but most conversation should be reserved for the nineteenth hole.

There is the slow player. She can turn a pleasant four hours on the golf course into a frustrating five hours. Two or three times her group has to stand aside and let another group play through. She has probably watched Nicklaus putting on TV and thinks if she just stands over the ball long enough it might go in.

Slow players may not even be in the player's own foursome. It may be a group ahead. They settle bets on the green, move slowly around the course, have an open fairway or two in front of them but never look back to see if they are holding anyone up.

There is the complainer. He is always finding fault with the course, or the greens are too fast or bumpy. He keeps talking about what he shot last week when the course was in better shape.

Then there is the referee. She is an authority on the rules. She knows them backwards and forwards and doesn't hesitate to use them whenever she can. I was playing with a friendly group when we came to a par-three. One of the group hit a good shot and I said, "What club did you use then?" This rules expert immediately said, "If he tells you, it's a two-shot penalty." He was right, of course, but it wasn't the U.S. Open. Another player of my acquaintance pulled a watch and timed a friend who was looking for a lost ball. That is, they *were* friends.

On the other hand, there are those who ignore the rules. They use the club head to move a ball out of a divot, they forget to count a stroke when they take an unplayable lie.

They miss a short putt and say, "give me a par on that hole, I would have made that putt if I really tried." The same golfer often also ignores the courtesies. He will tee off first even if he blew the last hole, and he consistently walks in another player's line on the green, leaving footprints just in front of the hole.

Then there is the self-appointed instructor. She makes suggestions to her playing partners, who may be beating her at the time. The usual statement is, "You looked up," or, "Slow down your backswing."

Wisdom of the World

I do not like thee
Dr. Fell.
The reason why I
cannot tell.
But this I know and
know full well.
I do not like thee
Dr. Fell.

Equally distracting is the one who is full of compliments. He constantly tells his partner how well he is playing, or "I wish I had your swing," and his partner gets so conscious of his swing that he loses all timing and tempo.

There are some people we just plain don't like. We cannot explain it. The pros have to play with anyone who is assigned to them, but the amateur usually can select her playing partners.

Fortunately, the opposite is also true. There are some people we enjoy playing with. Bobby Nichols said he was always glad to be paired with Ben Hogan because it helped him to concentrate. Many pros have expressed a desire to play with Sam Snead because they felt it helped them pick up his smooth swing. We all have people we enjoy playing with. It is what makes golf such a pleasant experience.

Obviously, the more we enjoy our playing partners the more we will be able to play with a quiet mind. Even so, there are going to be times when we play with people who create distractions. What is the solution?

Here we turn to the psychotherapists for help. They have certain basic principles that they use all of the time. The first is to recognize that all people are different. They approach golf, as they approach life, from a variety of different positions, not all of which we agree with. This is simply the way it is. To expect it to be different on the golf course is to live in a fool's paradise.

To put it in psychological terms, "Other people are going to act the way they want to act, not the way we want them to act." Other people have free will and they are going to think, talk, and act in ways that aren't to our liking, both on and off the golf course. To expect them to behave perfectly is to be irrational and to set ourselves up for frustration.

The most important thing that the psychologists have to say to us is that we can control our own response. As they put it, how other people think and act is their responsibility. How we respond is ours. Or they say, other people can't make you angry, only you make yourself angry by what you think or how you respond.

> **Wisdom of the World**
>
> *Remember, it is actually your thoughts that create your anger and not the other person's behavior.*[1]
>
> David Burns
> psychiatrist

When a golfer can recognize that she alone determines whether or not she gets emotional or frustrated and not what someone else says or does, there she has taken a giant step toward playing with a quiet mind.

[1]David Burns, *Feeling Good: The New Mood Therapy*. Wm. Morrow and Co., 1980, p. 167.

Second Conversation with Roland Harper

Dr. Charles Kemp: Let's pick up this conversation where our last one left off. In the psychological work that some of us do, we recognize that what a person says to herself has a real influence on how she feels and acts. We call it the "internal sentence theory." What we have been saying indicates that it influences her golf game as well.

Roland Harper: Definitely.

Kemp: Let's be practical. What should a person say to himself after he has hit a bad shot?

Harper: The hardest thing in the world to do is to forget the shot. That's like telling him not to think of pink. Suddenly everything in the world is pink. He should not say anything to himself about how to correct the swing. If he has hit a bad slice he should not say, "How do I correct a slice?" That's negative thinking. He should say, "How do I hit the ball straight?"

Kemp: What should a person say to herself when she finds she has a bad lie?

Harper: Again, don't say anything negative. She should

say, "I can hit a good shot out of a bad lie as well as a good one" or, "This is a challenge, I'll give it my best shot." Of course, it helps if you practice bad lies so you can say this with some confidence.

Kemp: Do you agree with the statement you can only have one thought at a time.?

Harper: There is no question about it. It only takes about a second and a half to make a golf swing. That only allows for one thought. Any more and it means confusion.

Kemp: How does a person eliminate extraneous thoughts?

Harper: It isn't easy. I knew a pro who had a drill that helped people do this. He would line up a dozen or so balls in a row and have the pupil hit one right after the other. This didn't allow for any swing thoughts or going through a check list.

Kemp: Then I assume you don't favor a check list?

Harper: No, only swing thoughts, and just one of those.

Kemp: The Pope was asked, "How many people work at the Vatican?" He answered, "Probably about half of them." How many amateurs really work at their game?

Harper: There wouldn't be that many. It would be less than 50 percent.

Kemp: Why doesn't the amateur see the value of practice?

Harper: It's not that he doesn't see it. In many cases it is a time factor. He has to give time to his business, he wants to give time to his family, to social functions. To really improve it takes about an hour a day, and they don't have that.

Kemp: Then he should accept his limitations?

Harper: Right.

Kemp: I understand you make certain demands of your pupils?

Harper: Yes, I don't set up a weekly schedule unless they hit a certain number of balls between sessions. I prefer five hundred to seven hundred fifty. I don't say I'll see you next Tuesday. If they hit five hundred balls in the next two days, I'll see them on Thursday. Then I am not supervising their practice, we are looking for ways to improve their game.

Kemp: Is anyone so good she doesn't need to practice?

Harper: Yes and no. In the beginning, no. When I was playing with Billy Casper, he didn't practice much at all. He would hit twenty or thirty balls and he was ready to go.

Kemp: I'll bet he did early in his career.

Harper: Sure, but once he had confidence in his swing then he would just play. Crenshaw didn't practice much, even early in his career, but he would go out and play thrity-six holes every day as opposed to beating balls on the practice tee. This may be the best method of all because on the course you aren't just repeating the same shot time after time. But again, the average golfer doesn't have the time to play thirty-six holes a day and has to use what time she can find to practice—that is if she wants to improve.

Kemp: Can a person practice the mental game as well as the physical? I mean, such things as imagination, concentration, etc.?

Harper: Yes, but it takes an enormous amount of imagination and dedication. It is much easier just to hit ball after ball. It means he must visualize hazards, distance, possible penalties, if he is long or short, etc., etc.

Kemp: One aspect of the mental game is strategy, what Hogan calls management. Cary Middlecoff says the difference between a player who uses good strategy and one who doesn't is about six strokes. Isn't that an exaggeration?

Harper: Only with good players. For people with handicaps of fifteen or more, it may be an understatement.

Kemp: Do you ever have people say, "I need help with my strategy."

Harper: Yes, more and more lately. Strange as it may seem, it is more common with younger players than with older ones.

Kemp: What are the points of strategy that you try to teach?

Harper: It begins on the tee—where you set the ball between the tee markers. I tell them not to try to hit the center of the fairway on every shot, but to place the ball where there will be the least penalty if they happen to miss-hit the shot. The same is true of the green. I want them always to think one shot ahead. That is the most common error in strategy—not planning ahead.

Kemp: Do you think most golfers should play bold or play safe?

Harper: Most of them should play safe. I see people try to make impossible shots out of the trees, across the water, etc., that simply can't be made. If they would play safe they would be playing bogey golf, then they would take it from there.

Kemp: Why don't teaching pros spend more time on teaching strategy and management instead of the grip, stance, etc.?

Harper: I think it is the students' fault. As I said earlier, some asked for it, but they are the exception. Most people want to know how to hit the ball a long way.

Kemp: How many amateurs do you think really know the rules?

Harper: About 2 percent. One hundred percent think they do.

Kemp: How many follow them?

Harper: Very few. Ladies do better than men.

Kemp: Is it that they are dishonest or just don't know the rules?

Harper: I don't think it is dishonesty in most cases. They haven't bothered to inform themselves. There are some who know the rules, but just don't want to be bothered.

Kemp: What rules are broken most frequently?

Harper: The two most common that I see are improving the lie and grounding the club in a hazard. They say the grass isn't good enough. The grass isn't very good at St. Andrews, the course where the game was invented, but they obey the rules there.

Kemp: I know. Once when I was in Scotland my caddie had to say to me. "No nudging please." What about the courtesies? Are they as important as the rules?

Harper: I think they are a part of the game. Golf is said to be a gentleman's game. It is important not only for yourself, but for those you are playing with and the ones who are behind you.

Kemp: What courtesies are the most important?

Harper: The one you hear the most about is slow play. That can be a problem. We have worked on it here at Colonial and our average round is three hours and forty-seven minutes. We have done this by making people aware of it. The other is not raking traps, not fixing ball marks, etc. I try to live by the motto, "Leave the golf course in better shape than the way you found it."

Kemp: I know you can teach people to play—that's been proven. Can you also teach people how to compete?

Harper: I do. I work at it. It goes back to the answers to all of your other questions. Play against par, not against your opponent. Know when to play defensively and when to be aggressive. Mechanically, it means to work on the short game. Most people don't want to be bothered with lessons on pitching and chipping, but that is where the scoring is done.

Kemp: What do you think it takes to become a winner at golf?

Harper: That's a helluva question. Certainly good ball hitting is not the answer. I know a lot of guys who can hit the ball great, but can't win anything. You have got to be clear about your objectives. I like to take my pupils to a par-three and ask them what their objective is. Invariably they will say, "To hit the green." I say, "No, that is not the objective. The objective is to make a three, whether you hit the green or not." You've got to be tenacious. Just as I've seen good ball strikers who couldn't win, I've seen some who don't have such good swings, but they will scratch and work and get their fours and fives somehow, while the other guys are trying to make perfect drives and good second shots.

Kemp: Do you agree with Curtis Strange when he says, "Everybody chokes"?

Harper: Yes, some say they don't but they are just as scared as the next guy.

Kemp: How do you deal with a player who says, "I've been playing terribly, what can I do?"

Harper: The first thing you have to do is discover what the problem is. Is she hitting the ball poorly or is she just not scoring? Nine times out of ten, it's scoring that is the problem. The place to begin with then is her short game.

Kemp: Do you think the average golfer expects too much of himself?

Harper: Definitely. We are too demanding of ourselves. We expect perfection. You just can't go for perfection and play good golf. There's no such thing as perfection even with good players. In any round you are not going to hit more than five to twelve good shots just the way you want them.

Kemp: What causes slumps?

Harper: Usually it is a lack of confidence that results in not hitting the ball well. A better question is, "What causes highs?" The modern expression is "being on a roll." A better word is that one's tempo is good. She's not swinging too hard or too easy. She's confident that the putts will go in. Then for some reason, she loses the tempo for awhile and has what she calls a slump.

Kemp: All the books say that tension is the great enemy of the golf swing.

Harper: I agree.

Kemp: How do you help people overcome tension?

Harper: Well, there are two kinds of tension, mental and physical. From the mental standpoint I think it is important to teach kids that they are going to have highs and lows and not to be too upset by it. I have watched Watson a lot and you can't tell whether he had a two or a nine on a hole. He just goes on the same way to the next hole. Hogan was that way too. Most great players are.

From the physical standpoint you begin with the grip. If the grip is too tight, that extends up into the arms, the back, the legs, the whole body. If you want to test yourself, just take a club and grip it harder and harder and you will feel the tension increase.

Kemp: All the studies speak of the power of the imagination. Do you teach your pupils to use their imagination?

Harper: Yes. You have got to imagine the flight of the ball before you hit it. The problem with some of my amateurs is that they try to visualize a shot that it would be impossible for them to hit.

Visualization is especially important in chipping and putting. You have got to see the flight of the ball, the bounce and roll on the green, and the path to the cup.

Kemp: How does the person you are playing with affect your game?

Harper: It differs with the players. I hear some say they can't play with poorer players, but I have to play with anybody. I can play with a 100 shooter or a 70 shooter. I play against par, not against the other player. Good players can play with anybody.

Kemp: Why do the pros say it is easier to come from behind than it is to lead a tournament?

Harper: I tell you what—they got into the lead because they were fairly aggressive, then when they find themselves in front they tend to become conservative and try to protect the lead. They begin to play defensively. When they are behind they have nothing to lose. For the weekend player, the same thing happens. When he realizes he has a chance to get a good score, he tends to become defensive and forgets what got him into that position in the first place.

Kemp: All the books say you have got to "just let it happen." What do they mean?

Harper: The truth is that that applies more to good golfers than it does to beginners or many amateurs. You can do that when you have confidence in your swing. It is a confidence factor. If you believe in your swing you can just trust it and let it happen.

Kemp: You mentioned playing in the zone.

Harper: It is a strange feeling. It's like a quiet walk in the park. You hit it, go find it, and hit it again without thinking too much about it. It just goes where you want it to go. But you can't plan on it.

Kemp: Just let it happen?

Harper: That's right. Just let it happen.

Postscript A

The Value of a Good Teacher

Ben Hogan, Byron Nelson, and Sam Snead were the three greatest golfers of their day. None of them was on a golf scholarship. None of them had the benefit of professional teaching. They all made a thorough, and in some cases an exhaustive, study of the game and practiced endlessly. This is no longer the case. The majority of winning golfers of recent years owe much of their success to the guidance of a college coach and the benefit of a good professional teacher.

Even Sam Snead relied on his brothers for advice and instruction. Way back in 1939, when he was having trouble in a tournament in Florida, he said he was going home for a lesson from his brothers because they were the only ones who knew his game. He drove all night to West Virginia, took his brothers out to the golf course, and took one swing. They both said simultaneously, "You're laying the club off and swinging flat." He looked at the club on the back swing, said "That's right, I am." He got back in his car, drove back to Florida, and won three straight tournaments.

A similar experience occurred in the life of Bobby Jones. It was in 1925, when he was playing in the Open at Worcester, Massachusetts. He was having trouble but didn't know why. Stewart Maiden was his mentor and, somewhat in desperation, Jones called him in Atlanta and asked for help. Maiden took a train at once—there was no air travel then—traveled to Massachusetts and watched Jones on the practice tee. After a while he said, "Why don't you hit it on your backswing?" and walked away. He noticed that Jones was rushing his backswing—end of lesson.

There is an old Scottish joke that appeared as a cartoon in *Punch* years ago. It pictured a golf pro talking to two middle-aged women. He asked, "Do you want to take a lesson, Madam?" She replied, "No, my friend does. I learned yesterday."

Probably the best known teacher-pupil success story is the lifelong relationship that existed between Jack Grout and Jack Nicklaus. Grout started working with Nicklaus when he was ten and continued to work with him regularly, even after he had won twenty major championships and dozens of other tournaments. He is recognized as the greatest golfer in the world, maybe the greatest ever, but he still went to Grout for instruction.

Another well-known pupil-teacher relationship is that between Byron Nelson and Tom Watson. It began when Watson was just coming into prominence. He challenged in a couple of tournaments but faltered at the finish. Nelson, who was doing the color on TV, sought him out after the

---

Wisdom of the World

Not only is there a great art in knowing a thing, but also a certain art in teaching it.

Cicero

Wisdom of the Fairways

It is this undying hope for improvement that makes golf so exquisitely worth playing.

Bernard Darwin

round and suggested that he was swinging too fast. This started a partnership that has developed into a mutual friendship, as well as very profitable instruction, and to a large part is one of the explanations of Watson's great success.

What was true of Nicklaus and Watson has been true of many others. Julius Boros worked with Tommy Armour. Bob Goalby studied under Johnny Revolta. Henry Ransom helped develop such fine players as Cary Middlecoff and Bobby Nichols as well as many others. Paul Runyan was the teacher of Chuck Courtney, Gene Littler, and Phil Rogers. Rogers has become a well-known teacher in his own right. He even includes Nicklaus as one of his pupils. It was Rogers who helped Nicklaus refine his short game a few years ago.

Harvey Penick of Austin, Texas, is recognized as a great teacher. Professionals on the tour call, write, and wire, seeking help. He tells them to come by and they often do. Kathy Whitworth credits him for much of her success, as do many of the good players on the PGA and LPGA tours. Two of the best known are Ben Crenshaw and Tom Kite, who started their careers under his supervision when they were at the University of Texas. They say that Penick never takes a negative position. He doesn't say what is wrong. He says, "I think you will do better this way," or "I notice the good players do it this way."

Also the touring pros frequently give lessons to each other. In the 1970 Colonial National Invitation, Homero Blancas was having trouble with his driver. Lee Trevino gave him a driving lesson the morning of the last round. That afternoon Blancas drove beautifully and beat Trevino by one shot. Trevino characteristically said, "a twenty-five thousand dollar lesson."

In recent years such teaching pros as Bob Toski, Peter Kostis, and Jim Flick are frequently sought out by touring pros to help them correct a fault or improve their game. There are very few self-taught pros of the Nelson, Hogan, and Snead variety any more. Lee Trevino and Calvin Peete may be the last of that breed. They came up the hard way and were largely self-taught. Good players now go to college on a golf scholarship where they get good coaching and competitive experience. Many of them were raised in a country club environment where they had excellent instruction at an early age from a teaching pro, and they continue to consult pros during their careers.

It takes talent to be a winning golfer, but in most cases it takes a good teacher to bring out that talent. The best players are aware of that and take advantage of every opportunity to benefit from it. As a result, they check their mistakes early and develop their full potential. Then, when they are ready to play, they can play with a quiet mind because they know exactly what to do. If touring pros who are the best players in the world feel the need for continued instruction, then amateurs who want to play well would do well to follow their example.

What does having a good teacher have to do with playing with a quiet mind? The best way to play with a quiet mind is to be completely sure of the fundamentals. The best way to become sure of the fundamentals is to have a good teacher who can train you in the first place and to whom you can return on occasion.

Postscript B

Faith: Secular and Religious

If a golfer is to play well, certainly if he is going to play with a "quiet mind," he must have faith. Superstars past and present, teaching pros, and sports psychologists all agree on one thing: Faith is an important ingredient if one is to play one's best.

Faith is a difficult term to define. It is used in one way on the golf course and in a different way in a church. Are there any common elements? What is the difference?

When superstars like Jack Nicklaus or teaching pros like Jim Flick speak of faith, they are talking primarily about faith in oneself. Faith on the golf course means that a golfer has got to have:

> Faith in her clubs
> Faith in his swing
> Faith in his decisions
> Faith in herself

The last point is the most important of all. Once when Ben Crenshaw's game was faltering he went to his early teacher,

Harvey Perrick, who said, "The first thing you have to do is start believing in yourself again."

It is precisely at that point, however, that the difference between faith on the golf course and faith in a religious sense emerges. The authorities all agree that a golfer must have faith in himself. They stress this over and over. In religion it is emphasized over and over that in the spiritual sense one does not have faith in oneself. One has faith in something, or someone, far beyond oneself. Faith in oneself is simply not enough for life's deepest questions and major concerns.

Wisdom of the World

It is faith in something that makes life worthwhile.
Oliver Wendell Holmes

Wisdom of the Fairways

You've simply got to have faith in yourself.
Many great golfers

There is a renewed interest in the relationship of sports and religion in these days. In post-game interviews, athletes frequently credit their success to their religion. The Fellowship of Christian Athletes is increasing every year, and numbers not only its members but its huddles (the name they give their groups) in the thousands. There is a Bible study group that meets regularly on the golf tour. Two of its better known participants are Scott Simpson and Paul Azinger. In 1987, one won the U.S. Open and the other was selected Player of the Year.

The relationship of religion and sport is nothing new. The apostle Paul frequently made reference to the sports of his day in his letters to the churches. In his first letter to the Corinthians he wrote, "Athletes exercise self-control in all things; they do it to receive a perishable wreath, but we an imperishable one" (9:25). He was referring to the olive wreaths they received as trophies instead of a wrist watch or a silver loving cup. He continued, "So I do not run aimlessly, nor do I box as though beating the air" (9:26). If Paul had been writing in the twentieth century, I have no doubt he would probably have used golf as an analogy to life instead of the Olympics of his day.

Golf has had a long relationship with religion. In the history of St. Andrews there is recorded an incident that occurred back in 1582 when a well-known archbishop was criticized for "disporting himself at the 'goffe' when he should have been preaching." The clergy have notoriously been fans of the game. One of the oldest of all golf jokes, which is recycled each year as a new story, first appeared as a cartoon in *Punch* years ago. It pictured an old Scottish preacher, replete in clerical collar and plaid Scottish cap, coming off the eighteenth green muttering to himself, "I'll hae to gie it up, I'll hae to gie it up." When they asked, "Do you really mean you'll give up golf?" he responded, "No, I'll have to gie up the meenistry." Almost every year someone says to me, "Have you heard the new story about the preacher who...?"

A long association with both golf and the clergy have made me aware of how much men and women of the cloth appreciate and enjoy the game. Perhaps this is one reason for so many golf jokes that have to do with preachers and religion.

What, then, is the relationship of golf and religion? That can be answered best by posing a series of questions.

What do we mean by religion? To attempt to answer that in a few words is obviously impossible. Libraries have been filled with books dealing with the question of the meaning of faith and religion. Needless to say, there are many expressions of religion in the United States. There are over two hundred different denominations, each with its own set of dogmas and beliefs. However, most religious groups agree on three broad general areas. Religion has to do with life's three basic relationships: with God, with oneself, and with others.

A person's relationship with God is one of obedience and dedication and faith. A person's relationship to oneself is one of sincerity, integrity, humility, and other such qualities of character. A person's relationship to others should be one of love and service. With other persons it requires the ability to be understanding, the capacity to care and on occasion to be forgiving, etc. It also has the larger dimension of being of service to others and to the world in whatever way a person can.

What does religion have to do with golf? It has the same thing to do with golf that it does with football, accounting, surgery, marketing, education, or any other area of life.

Is golf a religion? Some seem to think so. I appeared on a television show about the history and philosophy of golf at a local junior college. Several students were in the studio audience. Afterwards one of the students wrote a paper for a course on "Religions of the World." The title of the paper was "Golf as a Religion." Her professor sent me a copy. The first sentence read, "I will begin this paper with a definition of religion that is widely accepted today, given by the late Paul Tillich, who identified religion as that which is of 'ultimate concern.' People have been known to have ultimate concern for their automobiles, their professions, their homes, food, and yes, even golf."

In the sense that she was using her definition, this can be true. I have known some for whom it is true. But it is not true in the biblical or historical sense. In fact, this is what the Bible would call idolatry. This kind of religion has become a substitute for real religion.

Can religion help one play better? In the sense that religion frees one from negative emotions such as anxiety, guilt, and a lack of sense of personal worth, and enables one to live with a degree of serenity and peace of mind, yes, religion could help one play better golf. It would help a person perform better in any other human endeavor as well. It will not correct a poor grip or cure a bad slice. It won't even help one read the green better.

Will religion help one win? The next obvious question is, What if all players in a foursome are all religious? Which one will win? Azinger and Simpson both attend Bible study and both are big winners. What about the others who attend Bible study and aren't winners? Do Azinger and Simpson have better religion? What about those who don't attend Bible study but do win?

Dr. Robert Rotella, the sports psychologist that we have quoted so frequently, says that the psychological value of religion is precisely that it is not intended to help you win. Speaking of those who have a spiritual commitment, he says, "Less important than the peak experiences they say is the day-in-day-out emotional support that a deep religious faith can provide. The better job you can do separating self-worth from personal performance, the better off you're going to be....Playing on tour every week you get your head beat against the wall. The media tends to make only the guys who are winning feel good. But God doesn't care what you shot today, and that is exactly why it can help."[1]

We have said elsewhere in these pages that one needs to keep golf in perspective if one is to play with a quiet mind. Azinger says this is what his religion does for him. He says that when the pressures of a tournament begin to mount, he remembers that there are a lot more important things in life than winning or losing a golf tournament, even if it be the U.S. or British Open.

Scott Simpson says basically the same thing. He says that for him it is not the winning or losing that it deals with as much as his overall attitudes. He said his goal for the 1987 Open was to maintain an attitude of "contentment" regardless of the results. He said he keyed on a verse of scripture all week that reminded him to do his best—no matter what happened. (It was Colossians

> **Wisdom of the Scriptures**
>
> *Do not worry about anything, but in everything by prayer and supplication with thanksgiving let your requests be made known to God. And the peace of God, which surpasses all understanding, will guard your hearts and your minds in Christ Jesus.*
>
> Phillippians 4:6-7

3:17: "And whatever you do, in word or deed, do everything in the name of the Lord Jesus, giving thanks to God the Father through him.")

Golf is a game—a great game. Some of us feel it is the greatest game ever invented. It is a privilege to play it, but it is not a religion. All golfers want to play it well—and they will if they maintain faith in their swing, faith in their decisions, and faith in themselves. Then they will be playing it with a quiet mind.

Religion is not a game. It is a way of life, a way of faith. It deals with life's ultimate goals and values. It enables a person to face not only a game but life itself with serenity and peace of mind.

[1]*Golf Digest*. March, 1988, pp. 113.